Reflections in Muddy Water

Reflections in Muddy Water

LAYIN' DRAG ON LIFE'S HIGHWAY IN CASSVILLE, GEORGIA

Brad Stephens

To Heather:

Thank you for supporting Cassville and me!

ISBN: 1533483469
ISBN 13: 9781533483461

To my family, who put up with my talk about this book for ages.
To my friends, who put up with my stories at dinner parties.
To my sweet daughter, Elizabeth, who puts up a fight every time I change her diaper.

Preface

"Man, where are *you* from?"

That is a question that I have been asked a million times.

It started when I was in basketball camp in Spartanburg, South Carolina. The year was 1993. I was twelve years old and scrawny, and I had teeth so crooked that it looked like my tongue was in jail.

At the time, I was into my Air Jordans, the Red Hot Chili Peppers, *Saved by the Bell*, and a girl named Wendy. With my Walkman attached to my ears and my Orlando Magic Starter jacket on, I tried to play it cool. I was a 1990s kid through and through.

My jump shot was an impeccable back-spinning game changer, and my hair was shaped into a crew cut that made me look like an extra from *Hoosiers*. I could have been the great white hope, but my ball handling was suspect, and I could barely jump over a credit card. However, that did not stop me from trying to be the next Larry Bird.

Mom drove my brother and me over from Georgia to Spartanburg, where we would camp for three days. The first morning was filled with awkward introductions and a lot of sizing up—I had to see who had the best-looking Jordans and the quickest crossover.

After four hours of passing drills, the coaches announced it was lunchtime, and we all took our seats to annihilate the turkey sandwiches that our mothers made for us.

As everyone relaxed, we started talking about our hometowns. I gnashed my teeth, scarfing my cheddar and sour cream Ruffles while kids from Atlanta and Charlotte told stories about their subdivisions. It was swim meets, soccer teams, and minivans galore. Everybody's dad worked in technology and probably wore short-sleeve shirts with ties. Most of the mothers stayed home or worked part-time as personal trainers or a babysitters. It seemed wholesome enough, but I found myself yawning after the third story about a birthday party at a Braves game.

When it was my turn, I told them about my great-great-grandfather, one of the biggest characters who ever walked on the earth. He was a large man who carried $5,000 cash in the bib of his overalls, wore a straw hat, and was not afraid to take a swing at another man's face or to take a drink. A product of hard times and the Great Depression, Mr. Gus, as he was called by many, learned quickly how to survive, and he became very successful.

My favorite story was of him paying off an engineer to stop a train full of Crown Royal en route to Atlanta—so his hired hands could lift the loot and sell it to the thirsty citizens of Bartow County. One of those hired hands was a man I knew,

Mr. Adamson, who was in high school at the time. Mr. Gus marched into Cass High School, took Mr. Adamson and some others out of class, and paid them fifty dollars each to unload the boxes of Canada's finest onto his trucks.

Mr. Adamson once said to me, "Your granddaddy was not the kind of man you told no."

Mr. Gus was an entrepreneur of sorts and highly respected in the community. Like many people where he was from though, he had an edge. He was in church every Sunday, being part of the righteous Baptist congregation and singing "The Old Rugged Cross" with everybody else. The other six days though…it was another story. He wasn't a bad man at all, but you could find Mr. Gus buying a bull one minute and brawling in a bar the next.

After my nonchalant telling about the great train heist of 1949, those kids all looked at each other, turned to me, and asked that question: "Man, where are *you* from?"

One cannot properly tell the story of Cassville, Georgia, without describing the cultural landscape of the town itself. It would be like drafting a professional football team blindly and letting the players decide what position they want to play. You need parameters. A map of who, what, when, where, and why this little dusty corner of the universe is so special.

Located between Atlanta and Chattanooga, Cassville sits in the shadow of the big city and the Blue Ridge Mountains. While many areas around it have boomed in terms of population and economic growth, this little town has held firm in its one-horse state. If one were to drive through Cassville looking to spend the day touring museums and antebellum homes, they would be sorely disappointed. What they would find, though, is something much more special and far more entertaining.

Cassville may be nondescript to the ignorant eye and ear, but like many small towns in the South, it is sacred to those who call it home.

We are the children of the red clay—the ridge runners, the hillbillies, and the hicks.

Mayberry with an edge.

A place full of statistics—athletes who should have made it, those who could not "just say no," those who have been wards of the state, young people who walked away from education into a seedy existence, and drifters with unexplained pasts.

It is also home to gentlemen with impeccable manners, women so genteel that Scarlett O'Hara would call them prissy, hardworking souls who hit the ground running every day, kids who help old ladies across the street, foot-washing Baptists, college-educated folks who came home to make life better for themselves, and people who would give you their shirts off their backs and buy you coffee for good measure.

Cassville is unincorporated and has been since 1864, when William Tecumseh Sherman left it ablaze on his way to Atlanta. Legend has it that Cassville was going to be spared, but some townspeople thought it wise to slit a few Yankee throats in the middle of the night, and Cassville's fate was sealed. The town was almost completely destroyed. Prior to that, it was a bustling city with two colleges, a vibrant downtown area, and several thousand citizens, including several very prominent families with large homesteads.

The area suffered through Reconstruction, and the lifestyle enjoyed before was a distant memory in a flash. The railroads were destroyed by Sherman, and when the tracks were rebuilt, the railroad barons decided that a route through the neighboring town of Cartersville was more appealing. The future of the town took a massive hit because during that time, railroad depots were the heartbeat of commerce in the United States.

Jobs and people evacuated Cassville quicker than Herschel Walker's forty-yard-dash time.

Highway 41 changed the landscape for the better. Once the country became married to the automobile, the highway system snaked through rural north Georgia, and Cassville was once again connected to the outside world. Dixie Highway ran from Naples, Florida, to Detroit, Michigan, and Cassville was a stop for travelers headed north and south. My grandmother remembered waving to soldiers headed to parts unknown in 1942, their young faces seeing Cassville for the first time and probably the last.

The town came back to life in a way, but it remained quaint, and the population did not explode like it did in places like Cartersville, Marietta, or Dalton. Hotels, stores, and a few seedy after-hours establishments lined the highway all the way from Cassville to Adairsville, twelve miles north. These beer joints kept the police and local hospitals busy because, as one old man told me, "you'd get your ass [pronounced like *ice*] knifed in them places." While locals did not particularly approve, it helped the economy enough for blind eyes to be turned.

The 1970s brought another change that sealed Cassville's fate forever—the interstate system was finally completed. While it was a welcome sight for travelers, it was a death sentence for Cassville in economic terms. Interstate 75 was a giant asphalt marvel with no red lights and exits equipped with hotels, gas stations, and restaurants. The days of Highway 41 as the main vein of travel in north Georgia were over.

It was like Sherman ripped up the tracks and scorched the earth one more time. Within a few short years, most of the stores, hotels, and beer joints were history.

The town became sleepier than ever before. Three churches sufficed—two Baptist churches and one Methodist. One cemetery, Cassville Cemetery, served the area. Most of my family is buried there, along with three hundred unknown Confederate soldiers and General William Wofford, who was one of the last generals to surrender to the Union in 1865.

Most citizens worked in neighboring towns, opened their own businesses from their homes, or "loafed around," as my great-grandmother would say. (Loafing around is an art form—the ability to work hard at doing nothing is misunderstood. Some folks are so good at loafing that you almost have to give them credit.)

Cassville became a map dot, a destination that people only passed through and gave little thought. Most people define the borders of Cassville from various points along Cassville Road and simply going a mile in all four directions. Many towns across the South suffered a similar fate. There have been times when I have chosen backroads in Alabama, Mississippi, or Tennessee, and swear that I passed through Cassville at one point. A silence covered the area that has not lost its grip—one that is only broken by passing cars, lawn mowers, occasional gunfire, barking dogs, and the moaning of midnight trains.

It is a place where the wind blows and you can smell the chicken houses or jasmine, depending on where you are standing. Where roads are named after families long gone, either buried in the old cemetery or moved on to bigger and better things. The paved byways snake through pastures full of grazing cattle, meander among homes that harken back to a bygone era, and pass yards full of shirtless children riding bicycles in circles.

Pine thickets and giant oak trees provide the borders between single-family neighborhoods and trailer parks. The once-proud Highway 41 is lined by wild grass, cigarette butts, and broken hubcaps. Vagrants wander throughout the day and night, their purpose unknown and destination unclear. Sometimes, you can see their shadows moving in the night or materialize in your headlights and disappear in your brake lights as you pass them. There is a bemused sadness on their faces, as if they know something terrible but are afraid to share it.

A front porch is just as likely to contain human beings in rocking chairs as broken refrigerators serving as shelves for car parts. A yard can be perfectly manicured on one side of the street and look like the Everglades on the other.

These are the people that I grew up knowing—the families that held on through the years. The construction workers, backhoe drivers, farmers, mechanics, bankers, teachers, and loafers who called Cassville home.

In the midst of all the change after the Civil War, a small business located in a rickety wooden building held firm. Built in 1887, the town grocery store held on through the tough times, surviving everything from the Great Depression and the Great Recession of the late '70s to Walmart's assault on small-town USA. It never had a name until 1956, when it was aptly monikered Cass Grocery. It was around that time that my great-uncle RB Shinall purchased the property and took over the business.

RB was a beloved man in Cassville, and he was a total character. People used to call him "Sarge" because he would stand at attention behind the cash register most of the day. RB served in combat from 1944 to 1945 and was seen as a hero for helping to crush Hitler's Third Reich, like many men of his generation. Even today, the older people who recall RB always mention what a nice but tough guy he was.

RB died tragically on December 28, 1980. I was nine days old when they found him slumped over his steering wheel on Tennessee Street in Cartersville. For almost four years, the store was leased by his wife, Dot Shinall, until my dad purchased the property from her in 1984. After a few tweaks and a ton of help from my grandparents, Dad opened for business on September 1, 1984.

Cass Grocery took off from there. The store had always been a hangout for locals, a place where a Cassville man could take a load off and discuss the happenings of the universe over a cup of coffee and a freshly made biscuit. Dad made certain it stayed that way—a far cry from the interstate truck stops where you were rung up, cashed out, and shooed to the door like a naughty dog that got caught digging in the trash.

This collegial atmosphere set the store apart, and people took notice. The full-service gas pumps were a novelty that customers enjoyed, and frankly, as a long-time employee of Cass Grocery, I enjoyed it too. It was a great way to meet people, get to know loyal customers well, and let it be known that Cass Grocery was a friendly place where people were treated with respect. Dad would not have it any other way, and when I started working there, it was drilled into my head daily.

There were times where I swore those walls talked to me. The history of our little town was written on them and absorbed into the ancient wood. Those walls told the story of a place lost in the shuffle of modern times but surprisingly complacent with its niche in the universe. Sweeping up cigarette butts in the parking lot gave me a window to our little world that remains open in my mind forever. Southern Gothic with a mix of humor, hyperbole, drama, and a touch of fairy tale.

Ghosts of the past roamed the aisles, and those who remembered the souls who had come and gone made sure we knew about them. The old men, with their weathered faces from years of hard work, hard times, and memories of combat would tell their story as cigarette smoke encircled their heads like a supernatural crown of knowledge.

This is the story of Cassville—the people who ventured from the right and wrong side of the tracks to shop with us.

Those who piled into pickup trucks with Kool-Aid-mustachioed children to stock up on Fudge Rounds and Yoo-hoo.

The blue-collar and white-collar citizens who never let a day pass without stopping by.

The NASCAR fanatics who stocked up on beer on Saturday, only to run out on Sunday and beg us to sell them a twelve pack of Natural Light.

People with missing fingers from rodeo mishaps, band-saw hijinks, or drunken foolishness.

Women who could beat up men.

Alcoholics meeting us at 6:00 a.m. to buy a beer to stop the detox shakes before work.

All of them carving their niche in life, good or bad, for better or worse.

I moved on from Cassville after high school, and I have experienced life elsewhere. I lived in Athens, Georgia, for several years while I attended the University of Georgia, a wonderful place that the good Lord bestowed on the earth in 1785. I will be a Dawg forever.

After I got married, my wife, Laura, and I moved to Atlanta. There I was immersed in big-city life—high-priced coffee, sushi, traffic, people who could not name the members of Lynyrd Skynyrd, and parking decks that were ill suited for anything more than a Toyota Tercel. It was different, yet I can say my first foray into urban life was successful.

We also lived in New York City for three years. The cultural center of the universe. Despite the six-month winters, antigun laws, lack of crickets at sundown, and a basic view of the South that resembled the ending of *Mississippi Burning*, I thoroughly enjoyed my time in the Big Apple.

Throughout my years away from Cassville, I never forgot the people and the lessons I learned roaming the linoleum floors and asphalt parking lot at Cass Grocery. Their voices still resonated in my head. Their faces were burned into my brain, and when I missed home, I would think of them.

These characters shaped our town and changed my life forever. I have seen everyman, and let me tell you, he was all right in my book. I would not have the opportunities afforded me without the loyalty of these people and their fascinating, hilarious, and sometimes tragic way of life. I wrote this book in their honor and for Cassville—my unincorporated, un-Reconstructed, unrelenting home sweet home.

CHAPTER 1

Skizzleheads and Budweiser Keep the Lights On

WHEN DAD BOUGHT THE STORE in 1984, it consisted of three aisles of groceries, a milk cooler, one Coke cooler prominently displayed in the front, a Pepsi cooler hidden in the back, a deli counter, and of course, the main counter by the front door, where the cash register was located. The floors were a drab-brown linoleum that were immediately replaced with white tiles that breathed life into the sleepy little building.

Cass Grocery was one of those types of places that was never spotlessly clean. It was too old, too weathered, and too authentic to sparkle like the aisles in Target or Publix. There was always a coating of dust, a muddy footprint, spilled Coca-Cola, or tobacco refuse lying around. That was part of the charm.

The walls became adorned with ancient Coca-Cola signs and beer advertisements, shelves of antique bottles and tobacco tins, mounted wildlife, high school football schedules, and a giant band saw with a barn painted on it was on the wall behind the deli.

There was also the dreaded "bad check list" that Dad taped to the wall behind the register. This was the town scandal sheet and the names that appeared on the list became pariahs to us. Most customers would do anything to clear up a bounced check, but some would ignore our efforts to collect and end up with their name in black marker on our poster board.

A huge portion of the bad checks that we never collected had Bible verses on them. Sometimes Dad would read the verse aloud to me, slap the check down on the counter and say "if it was a tennis ball, it would bounce to Heaven."

The cooler in the deli was this white behemoth that weighed about seventeen thousand pounds. It contained all the meat any small town southerner would want, the most important of which was bologna.

Cassville people and bologna had a special relationship—they were as synonymous as funnel cakes and county fairs. It was like a bigger, less disgusting version of Spam and lent less credence to the question, Just what in the hell is this stuff?

The deli created a love-hate relationship with us. Slicing meat and making sandwiches was not a hard job, but customers could be picky or downright annoying. There was always one guy who wanted a pound of roast beef five minutes before closing. Slicing roast beef was like opening a shaken Coke in a Mini Cooper. A tidal wave of bloody juice would cover the slicer, the counter, the floor, and my hands. After cleaning the apparent murder scene on the slicer, we would finally get to leave twenty minutes late.

We also made hot dogs and barbecue sandwiches. The smell would emanate from the cookers and fill the store, making mouths water and men holler out "When is lunch?" at 8:30 a.m. Between my brother Matt and I, we probably ate thirteen thousand of those hot dogs during our childhood. The construction workers in the area would make a beeline to our door at noon to get "two dogs all the way" with a Coke.

The wildlife always drew oohs and ahhs, especially the bass my grandfather caught in Lake Hartwell. Its actual weight was nine pounds, and it was about a foot long. As time went by, the bass grew larger. By the year 2000, that bass weighed about twenty-seven pounds and was seven feet long. My grandfather caught it in a johnboat, probably shirtless, with a Merit cigarette dangling from his lips and a mesh-back Caterpillar hat barely perched on his head.

My grandfather was one of the most grizzled individuals that ever lived. Peepaw, as we called him, grew up in Byromville, Georgia with nine brothers and sisters. He left home at the age of fifteen, joined a CCC camp near Atlanta and then enlisted in the Army in 1940. In 1942, he left for Africa and fought the Nazi war machine until 1945, ultimately winning the Bronze Star during the Normandy invasion. He was a man's man and will always be my hero.

We also had a bobcat chasing a squirrel, two deer heads, two mallard ducks, and a rattlesnake coiled on a rock, with a random patch of fake mushrooms next to the serpent's tail. I told everyone that I killed that snake dead with one shot from my pellet gun. In reality, a guy needed cash, and Dad paid him fifty dollars for it.

NEEN

Neen was in charge of keeping the shelves stocked and ordering the groceries. She was my dad's mother and was affectionately known as "Miss Nancy" to most customers.

Every Wednesday, a truck from Cedartown, Georgia, would arrive at 4:00 p.m., and two guys would hand-truck totes of everything from Pine Sol to prune juice through our door and stack them up. Then we would hear the chorus of clicking price guns as we hurried to fill the shelves before the afternoon rush. We would arrange the rows of soup, flour, and cereal so neatly that Neen would get annoyed when a customer would buy something and mess up our handiwork.

"Looka there. After we got 'em all done, they come and rurn [ruin] it. Lord have mercy!" she would grumble.

Neen was the quintessential hands-on-her-hips, head-shaking southern woman who liked her electronic organ, cleanliness, homemade ice cream, soap operas, the *Price Is Right*, the Atlanta Braves, her privacy, and of course, me. Being her first grandson had its perks, and whenever I got in trouble at home, I would run to her house and get petted on.

"Your daddy is so mean. I'm gonna give him a talking-to when I see him tomorrow."

You did not want a "talking-to" from Neen. She just had an air about her that placed her above everyone, even though she was so humble. The customers went out of their way to be respectful of her. Foul mouths became angelic. Loud people went silent. Even the roughest people would always say "Hello, Miss Nancy" when she was at the store.

She was one of the few who called me "Bradley" and doted on me constantly, regardless of where we were or who was around. As my dad told me, "We all took a backseat when you were born." She was one of the best people I knew, a no-nonsense woman who always looked out for me and went out of her way for us no matter what. She would play "How Great Thou Art" on her organ for me, tell me stories about my late grandfather, and then watch QVC while I drank one of her homemade milkshakes on the couch.

She had short, curly gray hair and wore colorful button-down shirts and matching pants every day—she practically lived in Belk's clothing department. She refused to go to Atlanta, so if it could not be bought in Cartersville or Rome, then it was a nonissue for Neen. When I got my license, I offered to drive her, but she refused. "I ain't gettin' robbed down there with that bunch of heatherns." Crowds and traffic were her Kryptonite.

Her nightly ritual always fascinated me. When it was baseball season, I would walk down the hill to her trailer (she lived sixty-five yards away) to watch the Braves. She would greet me at the door in a robe and hair curlers, holding my customary chocolate milkshake. Gliding back to her rocking chair, she would plop down and crack open yet another diet Mountain Dew. Reaching over the stack of *TV Guides* on her side table, she would turn on her police scanner.

It could be the most tense moment of a Braves game, but if that scanner went off, Neen would instantly mute the game to hear the police banter.

"All units be advised—10-51 at 1925 Cassville Road. Be on the lookout for a white male, medium build, covered in blood."

Neen would shake her head and say, "That buncha trash over at the trailer park are drunk and fighting..." She knew every scanner code and address in the county. After the subject was apprehended, she would turn the scanner back down to admonish Bobby Cox's decision-making skills.

THE VICES

In 1986 Bartow County decided that being dry was for the birds and Mormons, so beer and wine licenses became available to those of us outside the city limits of Cartersville. To say my dad got his license quickly was like saying Herschel Walker could run pretty fast.

He literally was standing pat with nails in his mouth and hammer in hand. A walk-in cooler was constructed on the east side of the building and immediately filled with the golden nectar that made smart people dumb, scared people brave, and Cassville people magnify their inner caveman.

The addition of alcohol to the community was not without resistance. Dad was confronted by a couple of church elders who thought it unwise and immoral to keep a tool of the devil so close to their unsuspecting flocks. These were the same people who somehow drove the nicest Cadillacs or four-wheel-drive trucks while their congregations were clanking along in 1987 Ford Aerostar vans.

I think they underestimated my dad's lack of concern for their opinions and outright distrust of their self-righteousness. In no uncertain terms, these people were ushered out the door in the tone of "Don't let the door hit ya where the good Lord split ya."

Not being one to miss out on any vices, the Georgia Lottery Commission was created and called Dad a million times a week until he finally agreed to allow it in the store. There was a fear it would attract a bad element, but then again, it was Cassville. Bad elements were our thing. We embraced them.

The scratch-off tickets and online games rolled in the door, along with the depravity, self-loathing, and addiction that came with them. Men and women would come in, armed with their paycheck and lucky scratch-off tool, to decimate their bank accounts and relegate their families to a week of ramen-noodle dinners.

The scratch-off tickets were the real killers. "Lucky 7's" and "Jumbo Bucks" should have been called "Pain" and "Suffering." Players would win just enough to whet their appetite, but not before they threw enough cash into our register to pay for a road trip to Miami.

The online games had different effects on different people. Superstitious, dedicated people would play the same numbers every time and just shrug when they lost every week. The non-dedicated players would just let the computer "quick pick" their numbers.

The big game at the time was Mega Millions, with the jackpot starting at a paltry $2 million. Many of these players would only play when the money was at $10 million or more.

"Aw, man, you win that $2 million, you only get about $900,000 after taxes."

Good strategy. You lived in a single-wide trailer with a rotten redwood deck, drove a busted Ford Escort, and had three Chows chained to a tractor tire in the front yard—$900,000 would not help.

PVC Pipe and Such

Also that year, a hardware section was added to north side of the building. It was about three-quarters of the size of the grocery section and made up of four smaller aisles filled with automotive care products; paint; PVC fittings; door hinges; every nail, screw, and bolt known to mankind; and random items such as insulation, padlocks, electrical supplies, and toilet replacement parts.

Hardware was always good to us. It was a great rainmaker because people always wanted more than they really needed. Mr. Hummel down the street always needed another spark plug. Shorty Reed would come in to buy sixteen-penny nails and leave with two cans of red spray paint, a rubber mallet, and six feet of three-quarter-inch PVC pipe. The greatest thing about PVC pipe was the glue needed to affix fittings to pipe—no customers could *ever* remember if they had enough. We had to order two cases every two weeks because any time people bought fittings, I would remind them.

"Naw, I got plenty. Wait, do I? Hmmmmm. Aw, hell, how much is it, $1.99? Gimme two cans."

Customers in hardware were a mixture of the knowledgeable and the ignorant. Some intended to browse, and others were on a mission to get in and out as fast as possible. Picking out light-bulbs or hammers was not a difficult task, but anything involving busted water pipes, failing water heaters, rickety structures needing repair, or electrical work were grounds for marathon sessions trying to figure the where and why of lag bolts, wing nuts, heating elements, and plug wires.

Women in hardware were always an adventure. It wasn't that they did not belong, but the majority of females who traipsed into that section of the store had no clue what they were doing. It was like sending a bulldozer into a minefield. With hands on their hips and mouths agape, it was like dropping bread crumbs in a blind person's braille book.

Women never entered the aisles of the hardware on their own accord, either. It was an errand for the proverbial "he" in their lives. The "he" doing all the work back at home and who could not make it for one reason or another.

"He woulda come, but he's under the hood. I done told him not to buy that dang Camaro. It's a rattletrap piece of junk."

"He's been up on the roof all day with Randy and Johnny Huftstetler."

"He" would give her instructions, verbal or written, and send her to me. That was where the fun began.

The phrase "lost in translation" would apply as soon their shadows darkened my door. Nails, bolts, screws, and fittings became "doodads," "doohickeys," "whatchamacallits," and "thingies." In the days before cell phones, I could not tell you how many wasted trips were made by women who would try to explain what they needed with hand motions and rough diagrams drawn on my receipt book. It would look like a six-year-old tried to draw the dashboard instruments of the DeLorean from *Back to the Future*. The hand motions were always accompanied by "like is" and "like at," as if those words would suddenly clear the murky swamp that was their hardware knowledge, and we would find the "doodad that goes under that doohickey on the toilet...you know what I'm talkin' 'bout."

Once cell phones became common, I would end up calling the proverbial "he" under the hood or on the roof to find out what he was looking for. He would at least know the name, physical appearance, or on what aisle this clown car should be traveling. Before I would hang up, he would always offer a halfhearted apology: "Sorry, man. She don't know nothin' 'bout roofin' nails." (Ahh, thanks for clearing that up. I was about to send her to Home Depot to apply for a job.)

By the way, "he" was the second cousin to "they." The unseen know-it-all who spread propaganda and the lazy man who sent women to find car parts and bolts. These people caused more trouble at Cass Grocery than any customer who physically appeared before us. There was a proverbial "she" as well, but all she would do was send her man to get milk, bread, or toilet paper at the most inopportune times for him.

"Right in the middle of the got-dam race, and she comes in with a list of sheeyat she needs right this second. Little E's [Dale Earnhardt Jr.] in the pit, and here she comes. I swear I'm moving back to Fairmount and livin' with my brother."

I think this was payback for sending her to find wing nuts the week before.

Then we had the old guys in overalls who really did not need or want our help. Guys with names like Merle, Billy, Woody, Forrest, or Walter. They spoke another language, and anyone born after 1940 could not possibly understand it.

"I was plowing mah field, and mah Bush Hawg lost a skizzlehead, and it ran down into the Johnny key and fell into the crawdally. Y'all got any muddleskeets that go into a Billy shaft of a Bush Hawg?"

Even Dad would be lost on that one. I used to think they were making these names up, but then I would hear them discuss it on the benches. Their fellow overall-clad brothers in arms would offer their guidance: "Awwww, yeah. What you need is a filljacker that plugs into the fill line and connects to the hacknut on the drive shaft."

"Yep, you right, Earl. I hope they have one in there."

These men were like octogenarian MacGyvers and could fix anything with duct tape, pipe glue, and a pair of pliers. They never left the house without their pocketknives, $500 in cash, and a carpenter's pencil or tape measure. People of my generation with our "fancy phones" could not possibly help them do anything, ever.

CHAPTER 2

Exchanging Hubcaps and Alabama Largemouths

OUR DAY TYPICALLY STARTED AT 6:00 a.m. It was a whirlwind of activity as soon as Dad unlocked the door. Lights would come on, bringing the old building to life. The biscuits would start cooking, and the smell of bacon would waft through the air while my dad worked the spatula furiously. The worker bees, like me, would be running back and forth outside—turning on gas pumps, unlocking the ice machine, placing the seasonal merchandise out front for people to see. The first hour was always a race to get the store cranking, because the first customers were usually waiting for us at the door.

Dad ran the place with an iron fist. There was not much leeway with him, and it took me years to figure out why. A cash business had to be this way to be successful—there was no room for slacking off or letting anything slip. He did not take kindly to those who offered opinions about the business, chimed in on our prices, or generally carried a smart-aleck attitude. As Dad always told me, "You let somebody else run your business, you'll be outta business." He lived by this creed and never let up, which sometimes made the store a very unsettling place for him.

He was kind to people though. Dad gave credit accounts to people who could *never* get them anywhere else. He special ordered items for those in need, opened the store in the middle of the night for customers needing plumbing supplies, and always showed respect to the elderly men and women who had watched him grow up. People knew that, despite his serious disposition, my dad was a good man with a good heart.

While he was not one for humor at the workplace, Dad inadvertently made us laugh with his famous temper. Dad might be able to mask some things, but anger was not one of them. His eyes would bulge, his jaw would clench, and his face would turn a crazy radish purple. Nothing or no one was safe from the wrath of Dave. Property destruction was his specialty, and the best course of action was to duck, find somewhere else to be, or leave the premises immediately.

Price guns were complicated pieces of machinery that required tedious attention when they needed reloading. This was a nonissue for Neen, who had the patience of Job and the temperament of a Sunday school teacher. After all, she had played organ at the church for fifty years. That price gun could take two hours to fix, and Neen would hum "My Lord Is near Me All the Time" as she streamlined the labels perfectly. For hours and hours, she could also watch birds on her ten million feeders in her yard. Neen was the queen of yard art, and she enticed her feathered friends to land on her yard art so she could watch them.

Dad was a different story. You could see the sweat bead on his forehead as the roll of labels would unravel. You knew it was coming. The jaw would throb, and the face would change. The gun would shake as he tried to force the roll of labels onto the tracks, making matters worse.

A deep breath and a long, hateful stare before trying once more. The labels unraveled again and fell onto the floor. I sprinted in the other direction and randomly started spraying Windex on the cooler doors. That was my safe place.

Boom!

The price gun shattered on the wall, and the pieces flew onto the fountain machine, the coffeemaker, and the mounted bobcat chasing a squirrel. Dad paced back and forth as I wiped furiously and tried not to laugh.

"Brad! Clean that up!"

Dad picked up the phone, after uttering some choice words, to call the grocery delivery man.

"Hey, Mike. Dave Stephens. Look, one of my price guns does not work anymore...No, I don't know what happened to it. It just quit working. Brad threw it in the Dumpster, and they've already picked it up. Can you bring another one? Thanks."

Being a worker up there was a social exercise, a study in the functionality of rural southerners. It took a special person to handle all the hoopla. Dad usually relied on my brother and me, but over the years, he hired several guys who really did a great job. Local guys who knew the terrain and the nuances of Cassville life. Most of them were in their late teens or early twenties, old enough to understand certain things but young enough to say "Yes, sir" and "Yes, ma'am" with sincerity. Some of them were like brothers to me.

There was Jerry, who used to sing Eagles songs with me as we filled up Coke coolers. He would belt out "Take It Easy" without a care in the world. We traded CDs weekly (and I am sure I still have his Bob Seger *Greatest Hits* album in my basement). Jerry bought his first truck from my grandfather and spent eight years with us.

Rusty taught me how to tie a Carolina rig, fix a flat tire, and carry a hundred pounds of horse feed on my shoulder at age eleven. We spent hours working and fishing together, talking about women and what we wanted to do when we grew up. He was with us for about ten years, and I was in his wedding.

There were other guys who spent less time with us but had an impact on Cassville in their own way. The Parker brothers each spent two years with us and could pull the best pranks, including placing fresh roadkill in someone's vehicle. They both drove enormous trucks that you could hear coming from a mile away.

Cal was a big, jovial kid who worked with us when football season ended. He drove this tiny Chevy S-10 and I was certain he had to grease the door frame to squeeze in the cab. He was a few years younger, but I always considered him a friend because he was dependable and respectful. He went on to play offensive tackle at Georgia Southern and I got to see him play Between the Hedges in Athens once.

My cousin Keith worked with us part-time when he was not in his taxidermy shop. He was one of the few and proud men under fifty years old that smoked Lucky Strike cigarettes. We used to come up with naughty substitutions for the "L.S.M.F.T." (Lucky Strike Means Fine Tobacco) stamped on the bottom of each pack.

Greg was famous for reading the paper and watching TV during the busiest times. He was lazier than frozen pond water— but probably the most likable person who ever worked with us. Greg was also the most gullible and fell for any prank. He drank Mountain Dew most of the time, and once a week, we would fill the bottle with lemon dish soap. You could hear him groan "Aw, hell" and run to the toilet and vomit.

Then there was my brother, Matt. Both of us started our "careers" at Cass Grocery around the age of ten, stocking coolers and shelves for five dollars. As we got older, more responsibility came our way, and we were allowed to operate the cash register at age fourteen.

Being four years younger than me, Matt missed my first years up there but joined the fray in the late 1990s. He had endless energy, a sharp sense of humor, and no limits. His free spirit and constant movement made working with him an adventure. I have never seen anyone who could drink more Coke and still be functional. He was so scatterbrained one day that I counted seventeen Styrofoam cups in the trash. He would fill the cup about halfway, gulp it down in one swig, and toss it. I was certain the EPA would eventually show up and have him arrested.

No customer was safe from Matt's shenanigans. He would move people's cars after pumping their gas, and they would run frantically outside thinking it was stolen. He would shake people's drinks and laugh when it exploded in their faces, hide in the walk-in cooler and scream when someone would open the door, or make hot dogs with no wiener inside the bun. Rough-looking women would often get a Ric Flair "wooooooo!" when they drove by the store. Matt would stop cars at the intersection of Cassville and Cass-White Road simply to tell them how to get to Kingston, six miles away. Many of these people would drive away bewildered, rolling up their windows as quickly as possible as he ran beside them.

When I would question his motives, he would simply reply, "Pimpin'." People loved Matt and his personality. (He was and is the most fun person I know.)

There were rules, however. Dad would not tolerate rudeness, laziness, or being unkempt. Shirts were tucked in, and hair was combed or under a hat—and "always greet the customers as they come in." Failure to do so would likely get you cussed out or sent home. Dad had to be sure we set ourselves apart from the Walmarts and the truck stops of the world, as anything less would cost us our livelihood. If anything, Cass Grocery would be a friendly place, even if it was not the cheapest. For those of us who came of age there, it was like another classroom.

We all learned valuable lessons:

1) You didn't call elderly southern men "buddy."
2) A 1989 Chevrolet 1500 long-bed truck could handle sixty fifty-pound bags of horse feed.
3) You could exchange hubcaps on cars in approximately fourteen seconds. (My dad drove around with a Toyota Camry hubcap on his Chevy for about four days until he noticed it.)
4) If a woman caught her man with his girlfriend and she happened to have a piece of rebar in her hand, it was best to let them fight it out.
5) Nothing good happened on a payphone after 11:00 p.m.
6) There were some people who deserved free coffee for life; then there were others who should be charged for a cup of sink water, no matter what.
7) Milk jugs were like duct tape—they had many uses: milk, emergency gas can, collect charity at the front counter, noisemaker at a football game, and receptacle for muriatic acid bombs. (Take an empty milk jug. Add aluminum foil and muriatic acid, shake it up, and close the lid. Count to seven. The acid eats the foil and creates a gas that expands the jug until it explodes. It's the loudest noise outside of a Camaro backfiring in a garage.)
8) If there was a random half-empty bottle of Coca-Cola sitting around and you were unsure if it was yours, you let it be. It could be filled with dish soap, courtesy of your

coworkers, or it could be somebody's spit cup. (I know from experience.)

9) The three worst sounds you could hear—a tornado coming, a blown head gasket, and the deep sigh of a dishonest person about to ask you for credit.

10) If somebody over the age of twenty-five rode a bicycle to the store every day, he or she probably did something really bad or stupid recently.

Dad taught us how to pump gas, check oil and transmission fluid, make keys, cut screen for windows and doors, help people figure out the most convoluted of plumbing and/or construction issues, stock coolers and shelves, and most importantly, how to deal with all the personalities.

For every nine-to-five person who had it all figured out, there would be someone who was on parole. For every kid who played sports and minded his or her manners, there was one who cussed out teachers and started smoking at age nine.

My generation was indicative of this paradigm—my high school class suffered over 60 percent attrition from ninth to twelfth grade. When I returned to school after the summer breaks, dozens of people would be missing, as if they vanished from the earth. Some of those people lived less than five miles from me, and I never saw them again.

The parking lot could hold about five cars. Two more could park next to the pumps, and two more could park on the south side of the building, and others could park across the street in Mrs. Allen's empty lot. She was one of the sweetest people on the planet and allowed our customers to park there for free. I think she missed church twice in seventy-six years, and she could recite any Bible verse in King James–style with all the "yeas" and "begats" you could handle.

Mrs. Allen lived next door to some rough people, or "heatherns," as she and Neen called them. The kind who slept all day and wandered around looking for trouble all night. The men never wore shirts. The women never wore shoes, and they smoked Marlboro Reds with their babies in their arms. The yard was never mowed, there were at least two inoperable vehicles in the driveway, and the screen porch looked like it had been in a fight with a Weed eater. During a drug raid, I saw a cop slam one of them on the hood of his inoperable Mustang.

Not once did those people ever cross Mrs. Allen. This tiny, cotton-topped lady commanded respect from even the worst people. I was certain that if they had messed with her, God would have rained fire and brimstone on their houses until they were piles of ashes. She and my great-grandmother were best friends, and Mrs. Allen would call our house every time she noticed one of the outside lights at the store burned out.

PARKING LOT DAYS AND SILENT NIGHTS

That parking lot was the scene of so many fights, dares, bets, layings of drag, and clandestine deals that the local police could have moved a precinct across the street and filled the jail. The pay phones on our property attracted a sordid, seedy underworld that we often had to watch closely.

Cars would pull up beside each other, and men in cutoff T-shirts, clearly discussing world events and stock options, would whisper to each other while they leaned up on the hood. Then they'd go to the pay phone, page someone, and lean back on the hood to await the ring. As soon as the first ring came through, these men would spring off the hood and grab the receiver as if it were Publishers Clearing House ready to give them a check.

At least once a month, we would have to tow a vehicle left overnight. I remember a baby-blue Camaro that I had towed when I opened one Saturday morning—the passenger seat was slowly burning from an abandoned cigarette, and a Louisville Slugger was slammed through the windshield like a spear. The backseat was covered in *Hustler* magazines and an empty dog cage. Somebody either had an awesome party or was party to animal cruelty (I guess nobody will ever know).

The east side of the store was where we stored the PVC pipe, potting soil, pine straw, and fertilizer under a large makeshift tin roof. Weeds and broken pieces of concrete carpeted the ground back there, along with a million cigarette butts and empty Coke bottles. It was protected by a chain link fence with barbed wire around the top, in case any mischievous Cassvillians decided to steal some 10-10-10 fertilizer in the middle of the night.

Two young boys from a local trailer park hopped our fence late one night and tried to kick the back door down. Unfortunately for them, the door was made of thick steel, which made their attempts as futile as a fire ant stinging an elephant.

A loud thudding noise echoed every time their feet slammed into it. The commotion drew the attention of the Petersons, who lived next door to the store and were usually up at all hours of the night, due to the husband's work schedule and the wife's meth habit.

The cops were called and the deputy snuck up on the would-be burglars with his flashlight. He shined it on them and told them to stay put. The boys took off in a sprint into the black night to avoid the deputy, but clearly forgot they jumped a fence to get in there. They hit the fence at full speed and knocked themselves out cold.

More often than not, we would be running back and forth to the gas pumps, under the tin roof, and back inside without stopping for several hours. I would be covered with dust, sweat, pine straw, and 10W-30 oil stains. When I would get home, Mom would remind me of how awful I smelled.

Other times, it would be so quiet that you could lay down and take a nap on Cassville Road. The fan above the deli would spin in slow motion, and you could almost see the taxidermy move on the walls. Random customers would walk in, their cigarettes dangling from their lips, and the smoke would hang in the air for what seemed like hours.

In the winter, when it would be dark by 5:00 p.m., the only sound outside was the train blowing its mournful horn on Peeples Valley Road three miles away. The old radio, usually tuned to South 107 out of Rome, would faintly play a Vince Gill song as the sun went down behind Mr. Delano's house across the street. Dad and I would prop up on the bench outside, share a glass-bottled Coke, and talk about Georgia's recruiting class for next football season.

Dad finally put a television behind the counter in the mid-1990s. He was always concerned that it would distract us from our work, but it was necessary. The channels were limited, but frankly, we only needed two. Normally, it would be a fishing show until Dad decided he wanted to watch the news. Names like Shaw Grigsby, Bill Dance, Dean Durham, and Jimmy Houston reverberated off the walls of Cass Grocery all day long.

Dad could not have cared less about such things. He was obsessed with the news and could leave it on political talk shows all day. As soon as his truck pulled out of the parking lot, the channel would instantly change. None us could understand how Dan Rather was more interesting than Denny Brauer.

Crisis in the Middle East? Nah, we would rather watch an Alabama largemouth get snagged by a Rooster Tail on a baitcaster.

However, we did not need a television to be entertained. There was always mischief to get into or one of our customers telling us a farfetched story that involved jail time, drag racing, a fist fight, and a random truck stop in Carrollton. This could happen at any time.

Mr. Simpson was an old man who restored and raced 1950s-era Chevrolets all over the United States. He used to tell us stories of racing at the Bonneville Salt Flats in Utah, meeting some Indy-car drivers, or partying with women half his age in a hotel in Chattanooga.

He ate at the Waffle House every morning and every night. Around 6:00 p.m., he would venture up to the benches to eat two Honey Buns and drink a quart of chocolate milk. My dog would always get excited when Mr. Simpson would come around, because he would buy half a pound of sliced bologna to feed to him. Then he would start up. "Boys, this one time, I was in this bar outside of Cullman, Alabama…"

My dog was a source of merriment for many customers. Joe Duke Montana was the greatest Airedale that ever lived and truly man's best friend. Weighing over 100 pounds, Joe was a hairy, four-legged mascot that adults and children fawned over while he wallowed on the dirty ground like a rug with huge teeth. His stubby tail wagged incessantly as he was fed everything from gummy bears to potted meat.

Considering the smorgasbord he was fed by our customers on a daily basis, he refused to eat dog food. Our table scraps became his food source at home, which Mom placed in an old sauce pan under a giant pine tree. He would tear out of his doghouse and engulf chicken bones, sweet potato skins, fatty parts of red meat and uneaten vegetables that I could not fathom putting into my mouth.

Joe was very territorial. If another dog came into our yard or up to the store, it was like drawing a line in the sand. Airedales have the largest incisors of any dog on earth and Joe was not afraid to sink those teeth into any canine that dared to intrude on his property. There were no inside dogs or leashes in Cassville and Joe maimed more than his share of wayward Chows and Labrador Retrievers. Our neighbor's mutt was the only exception.

This mutt followed Joe around everywhere, like a remora attached to a great white shark. He was Twenty-Five pounds of fat with stubby legs, which lead to his owners calling him Roley. He would nip at Joe's paws, jump on his back, bite his tail and bark right in his face. They wallowed in the fields of wild onions together and would come home smelling like the wrath of God.

One summer, I spotted Roley devouring our table scraps in Joe's pan. A giant ribeye bone was there for the taking and Roley was gorging as quickly as he could.

"You are taking your life into your own hands. He is watching you from somewhere," I said.

Joe never budged. I guess he needed one dog friend that did not run from him in terror. He never allowed Roley to take part in his buffet at the store, though. Roley could only watch as Joe pigged out and snoozed in the shade while the grizzled old men rubbed his head.

On slow days, we would be hanging around, doing necessary cleaning or shooting the bull. A car would pull up, and one of our best customers would get out with a black eye, a limp, or just a twinkle in his eye. He'd walk in with a grin, grab a twelve pack of Natural Light, an Oatmeal Creme Pie, and some Goody headache powders.

He'd point behind us. "Gimme two packs of mah cig'rettes too, man."

We'd grab the packs and turn to the counter, and he'd say the line that made so many men in Cassville famous (and notorious): "You ain't gonna believe what happened to me last night..."

RACE RELATIONS AND TORNADOES

No book about the South is complete without these two topics. They may be mutually exclusive, but these topics are intertwined in southern literature like whackings and cannoli in *The Godfather* trilogy.

Cassville never had much of a race problem when I was growing up. Black folks were just as welcome in our door as anyone. In fact, it really was not something I thought about until I went to middle school and heard racial slurs for the first time. It was just not part of the equation at the store.

When I was in elementary school, I used to sit outside on the benches before school with a black man named Lamar. He worked first shift at a carpet mill, and his ride to work would pick him up at the store promptly at eight. Lamar always showed up with a shower cap on to keep the lint out of his hair. On cue, I always asked, "Lamar, why you always wearin' a shower cap?"

"Cuz I's dirty, boy!" He would cackle and flash a smile with a gold tooth in the front. The old men would smile and tell Lamar to "take it easy, and don't work too hard" when his ride arrived.

There was the blind piano player who lived down the street who kept a credit account with us. He played for the Baptist church across the highway, where the black folks attended. He walked up to the store every day and bought a pack of Kool Milds and sometimes a spark plug or two for his lawn mower. Somehow, this man figured out how to safely walk the street, walk behind his lawn mower, and play piano without his vision. On Sundays, he would bring his paycheck from the church, and Dad would settle his account by cashing it.

A lady named Diana had a catering business that was very successful. Every July 4, she would cook hundreds of steak dinners for people all over the county. I worked every July 4 that I could because people were in a good mood, and I didn't mind making the money for a whole day. Once the catering deliveries were done, her assistant, Mike, would drop by with a hot plate for all of us. The only charge for those tasty morsels would be a carton of Basic cigarettes, which we had sitting on the bench waiting for him.

Mike was one of my all-time favorite customers. He was in his midforties, worked about twenty-seven different odd jobs, and wore the same three shirts for about twelve years, one of which was a "Makin' It" T-shirt. Mike had a loud voice, and his laughter would shake the walls as much as his giant belly. He would come strutting into the store and tell some of the wildest, X-rated stories in the history of mankind to make us laugh.

The man had no filter, but he did have respect. He walked in one day and railed off some farfetched, profanity-laced tirade about carnal knowledge of a local woman. When he finished, I looked behind him and said, "Hey, Neen."

Mike turned white, and his jaw dropped. He turned quickly to find nobody, as Neen had gone home to tend to her yard art.

"Maaaaaaan! You can't be doin' that! Miss Nancy knows my mama! If she heard me talking like that, mama'd slap the hell outta me!"

Then there was Miss Fannie Lee, who once slapped her forty-five-year old son in the face for using profanity in the store. She spun him around, popped him hard, and said, "You ain't been raised to talk like that!" As his lip quivered, she glared at me and said, "Give me two boxes of my snuff." Several of the elderly women dipped Bruton and Dental Mild, which might be the most disgusting single thing on the planet.

Black folks came and went in our store daily, just like anyone else. I could not recall one incident of trouble in my entire life, and strangely, I hadn't (and still haven't) laid eyes on a Klan robe. Those who buy into the national perception of South would be sorely disappointed if *TMZ* or *Nightline* showed up in Cassville to do an exposé on race relations. The only thing they would find would be old men sitting around smoking and talking about the weather, young white and black kids playing sports together, and this occasional question, posed to me or my dad: "Yo, man, can I hold a pack of Newports until I get paid on Friday?"

The answer was always yes.

The other national perception that plagued (and still plagues) the South was our fear of and propensity of tornadic activity. It was no secret—there had to be a magnet in the northwest Georgia soil that drew tornadoes out of the sky and into our lives. Hell, just about every spring of my lifetime had been marked by a twister touching down somewhere.

Whether it was the telltale freight train sound, the smell of snapped pine trees, or the sickening feeling of helplessness, this weather phenomena was often no laughing matter. Lives were lost, property was destroyed, and millions of dollars went down the drain trying to rebuild from the wreckage.

However, the aftermath often drew out the people that Jeff Foxworthy so eloquently described years ago. Field reporters never interviewed anyone with a functioning brain. It truly was the lady in the muumuu and hair curlers. Every town in the South had one, and Cassville was no exception.

A tornado touched down one afternoon in the late 1990s, about one mile north of the store, and everyone in the area passed the word that several homes were destroyed. I got off work at 4:00 p.m., and being a shameless rubbernecker, I headed north in my truck to survey what "the finger of God" had done on Cedar Creek Road.

News crews were parked on either side of the road, fire trucks were in the driveways, and Georgia Power linemen were chain-sawing tree limbs. A double-wide trailer was peeled open like a can of tomatoes, and somehow, the inoperable Camaro in the front yard was picked up and thrown upside down into it. The family survived, due to their storm shelter, and the news reporters were eager to talk to them.

As I looked at the family in their sorrow, I could not help but shake my head. The barefoot husband wore overalls with no undershirt, had bare feet, and wore a mesh-back Bill Elliott hat. The wife had on a pink muumuu and house shoes and a shower cap. Their three kids were running in circles around them as they talked to the reporters, sword fighting with tree limbs from the sweet gum tree that lay on top of their living room. Not a one of them wore a shirt.

I heard the man remark, "I said, 'Hell, Wanda, it's a-comin' a tornader.' She runned out the door, and I throwed them kids down in the shelter just as the Camaro went in the air. First time it's moved since 1992. He-he."

Every yard was filled with families with exactly the same appearances, ready to talk. One man was missing six of his ten fingers, sitting in a lawn chair in his pajamas, smoking a cigarette. The feeding frenzy among the reporters was like a herd of sharks attacking a chum pile in a baby pool. I am sure that afternoon set Cassville back about thirty-five years in the eyes of America.

Of course, there was always one man in every family who survived a tornado by being tied to a tree stump. Despite the fact that I never met a single one of these brave men, that story never died out.

CHAPTER 3

"Growed" Kids, Cigarettes, and Bar Fights—the Benches of Cass Grocery

COFFEE SHOPS WERE NEVER A part of my life until I went to college. I actually never darkened the doors of a Starbucks until my senior year of high school, when some people decided that we needed to finalize our prom plans over coffee in Kennesaw, about thirty minutes south of Cassville. Kennesaw was a busy city with giant car dealerships, every restaurant in the known universe, and Town Center Mall, the shining beacon of light for addicted shoppers of northwest Georgia. For seventeen-year-old males, it was prime hunting ground for unsuspecting females who were more concerned with the 25 percent off sale at Wet Seal than riding around with us.

In any event, Starbucks was like another world. There was jazz on the speakers. People wore scarves for no apparent reason and read books about the French Revolution while ordering such foreign substances as "latte" and "macchiato." I ordered a hot chocolate and surveyed the landscape as we sat down. Snickering to myself, I imagined my people from Cass Grocery trying to order a "triple soy vanilla latte with extra foam" without giving up and proclaiming Starbucks "a bunch of smartass liberals."

We were ducks out of water, and it was clear. My friend Daniel sat down next to me and promptly hit the table with his knee, covering his lap and mine with his hazelnut latte. He let out an "Aw, sheeeyat," and the other people looked up from their discussion about Emily Dickinson to see us scrambling around. The John Coltrane song on the radio went silent. We were like aliens who landed on Earth, and as the earthlings gathered around our flying saucer, we all fell down the extended staircase.

We finalized our prom plans at the Waffle House instead— I'd take a scattered, smothered, covered, and chunked hash brown over a latte any day.

When my dad took over the store in 1984, he ensured that a Cass Grocery tradition remained intact—the benches attached the front of the store. It was like stadium seating for the awesome theater that was life in Cassville, inhabited by generations of Cassville men from all walks of life. The benches were like a gentlemen's club, where coffee flowed freely along with opinions, feelings, knowledge, gossip, and some of the biggest whoppers ever told.

(For the ignorant, a "whopper" is not a burger in Cassville. It is a massive lie that is obvious, but nobody feels the need to stop the storyteller. The whopper needs to be told so the other men can repeat the whopper elsewhere and claim firsthand knowledge. Never let the truth ruin a good story.)

The benches were made of wood and conveniently located by the front door, facing Cassville Road. On the left side were two levels about six feet across, where at least four people could sit comfortably. The right side of the door had two levels that were fifteen feet across, allowing room for ten to twelve men to sit down with their coffee and cigarettes. It was a perfect view to the road, the parking lot, and the gas pumps.

At any given time, there could be two to twenty men sitting or standing around out there. A cloud of cigarette smoke, coffee cups, and aluminum foil wrappers from their biscuits would adorn the front of the store as they engaged pressing topics, like who got arrested on Cedar Creek Road last night, or who was the best backhoe operator in Bartow County? No matter how enthralled they were, they would always speak to people they knew who were coming into the store.

"Hey, Curtis, how's your brother doin?"

"Gloria, tell your daddy I'll be down 'nair after lunch to measure that doorframe."

"You keepin' 'em in line down at Cedartown, Bobby?"

Becoming part of the bench crowd was tough though. Those who did not pass muster were ignored or met with a "do what?" attitude when their unwanted voice interjected into a spirited discussion about the price of copper tubing in 1976. The following rules and criteria had to be followed to gain admission to the bench crowd.

First, you had to be over forty-five. That was old enough to have worked a long time, to have gone through a divorce, to have kids that were "growed," and to refer to "back then" without sounding foolish.

One guy, Eddie, so badly wanted to be included, but he flunked this portion of the test. I was talking to a group at the benches about a fight I saw in school. The two kids had been suspended for a week, even though only one punch had been thrown.

There was a sarcastic "humph," and Eddie remarked, "Back in our day, that ain't how it was done, right, boys?" He glanced around at the old faces, cigarettes dangling from their mouths. Eddie fully expected something like this: "Naw. Them teachers would have took us out in the back and let us fight it out. My daddy woulda knocked my head if I didn't…"

The problem was that Eddie was maybe forty at the time.

Will, one of the more respected members of the group, said, "Eddie, what you talkin' 'bout? You were still in diapers when I was dodgin' shrapnel in An Loc, boy."

Translation: You were the weakest link. Good-bye.

The older you were, the less validation you needed to be included. In the South, we were taught to respect our elders and that sentiment never died. I always loved that when the oldest guys would show up, the others would just sit and listen to them talk. Interruptions were common out there, but not when the really old guys would pop in and "sit a spell." Nobody's opinion mattered more than a seventy-five-year old World War II veteran who had worked as a mechanic for thirty-six years.

When those old guys would finally wrap it up and head home, the stories about them would circulate around the bench.

"Ol' Andy, I swear, they don't make em like that no more…"

"Andy fixed my backhoe for free, but Wanda gave him a whole Winn-Dixie bag of 'maters anyway."

"Andy got in a fight at the VFW bar back in the seventies. Somebody threatened to knife him, and Andy beat the tar outta him with a chair. Didn't even get arrested. Turns out that other'n didn't even serve. He was somebody's cousin from outta town. Thought he was tough. Ol' Andy learned him though…"

Honestly, any veteran of combat was held in high regard there. So many men I knew served in Vietnam. There was always a tinge of sadness behind their eyes, as if they let the country down because the war was not seen as a success. They are my heroes and will always have my undying respect.

There was Will, who did a thirteen month tour of duty from 1967-68. Jerry, who helped my cousin at his taxidermy shop, and Randall, the plumber who fixed up the store and our house when things went wrong, were forward scouts for the Army. One of my youth basketball coaches had a brother killed in south Vietnam in 1969.

Then there was Mr. Lee, who was a lineman at Georgia Power and always ordered a slaw dog from our deli. He was surrounded by the NVA with thirty-two other Marines on a no-named hill near Khe Sanh in 1968. There was no hope for relief or reinforcement. After hours of vicious fighting, he and three other survivors were airlifted back to their command post. He was wounded three times and sent home after several surgeries. That story still haunts me to this day because I could see Mr. Lee's kind face turn ashen as he told me about it.

Being a good listener, I noticed many of these stories would change up every time they were told. I knew to keep my mouth shut though. Honestly, sitting out there every day with them—I was convinced that the toughest, meanest, smartest, and most honorable men in the world came from Cassville.

Second, no women allowed. Period. End of story. This was the He-Man Woman-Haters Club in mesh-back hats.

Every now and then, their wives would show up at the store while they were hanging around, and it would change the entire dynamic. It was not a welcoming environment.

The bench was where these men would retreat to discuss fishing, politics, sports, fights they witnessed or took part in, car repairs, horror stories about going to Atlanta, and of course, how awful their wives and kids could be. This bench was their Augusta National, and the green jackets were not handed out to just anyone, but especially not to women.

The appearance of the wife would bring a look of dread and disgust. The other men would not comment on her, as that broke protocol. Only her man could refer to her in a negative light, nobody else. They would simply nod in agreement and drag on their cigarettes as he would rail on and on: "Aw, shit. Here she comes. I bet my honey-do list is a damn mile long. Why can't she just stay at home or wait till I get back? Ugh. She gonna make me go to town—I just know it."

("Going to town" meant a trip to Cartersville, six miles away. However, this six-mile jaunt might as well be six hundred to them. Going to town was a dreaded journey, the bane of their existence, and to hear them tell it, Cartersville was a crime-ridden, overcrowded urban nightmare. The only thing worse was going to Atlanta—which was hell on earth and at least 1,298 miles away.)

I gave the wives credit though. Most of the time, they would just come into the store, make their purchases, and leave with a "see you at home" to their men. There were times, however, that the honey-do list would be read aloud to him in front of his friends. This was akin to emasculation and opened the door for the other men to pile on.

"Ha-ha! Tony, we know who wears the boss pants in your house now."

"Better get to steppin' and fetchin' there, sweetheart."

"I can hear that whip crackin' all the way up in Darsvull [Adairsville]."

The only two exceptions to this rule were my mother and Neen. Mom got a free pass because Dad owned the place, so they always greeted her with a smile. In fact, everyone greeted my mother with a smile. Mom taught in the county school system for thirty years and knew just about every single human being in the state. Universally beloved, she never was in a bad mood and had this inviting nature that made people happy. She took care of us with the patience of Job and endured our foolish behavior with constant laughter. Although she rarely stayed at the store for more than ten minutes at a time, our customers always asked, "how is that sweet momma of yours?"

Neen worked with us, and those guys all loved and missed my grandfather, so Neen could sit down on the benches anytime she desired. (Not that she needed their approval. Neen would have sat down anyway.)

Third—and this was of utmost importance—if the rules were not followed here, invalidation would be instantaneous and brutal:

A) No T-shirts could be worn unless it was Sunday or over ninety-five degrees.
B) Absolutely no shorts, ever.
C) You had to own at least one cap that you received for free from buying a piece of equipment.
D) Flannel shirts with at least one pen in the pocket, along with the tobacco product of your choice, reading-glasses case, or receipts from buying plywood or other various construction necessities.
E) Boots every day unless it was Sunday. On Sunday, tennis shoes were acceptable, but no fancy running shoes—plain white or plain black only.

Breaking these rules would certainly indicate you were not one of them. There were very few exceptions made, and I witnessed the turnout of several potential members of the group. It was a subtle exclusion—his voice was no longer heard, and his presence had no impact on the others.

Bill was one such turnout. Bill was not an original member, but he assimilated pretty quickly upon moving to Cassville. For a few months, he could carry on a heated discussion about sprinkler pipe or carburetors with the best of them, and the guys would listen. Bill was in his midfifties, wore flannel, was usually dragging equipment behind his truck, and smoked one cigarette after the other. Totally perfect...until June of that year.

He started wearing shorts and tennis shoes every day.

In the face of pointed questioning, Bill became defensive and did not change his ways. He blamed the Georgia heat, which was no defense for lifelong Cassville natives, who had always seen hotter days. Regardless of how hot you said it was, there was a day in 1973 that was hotter. Always. (Just give that up right now.)

This also applied to tornadoes, bar fights, getting pulled over for speeding, and barbecuing. No matter what you had encountered—another's tornado experience was worse, the bar fight was more destructive, he was driving faster when the cop stopped him, and the barbecue he had was much tastier. No contest.

Bill became a pariah. Persona non grata. He was like the kid screaming "Hey, look at me!" as the circle would close with him on the outside looking in. All he had to do was don his Wranglers and Justins—the issue would have been resolved. As such, when Bill would leave, the truth would come out.

"Bill done got weird on us. You know he was born up north, right?"

"I got tard [tired] of him braggin' on his boat anyway."

"He puts cream in his coffee too." (Shaking head in condescending disgust.)

Wearing flannel was a big-ticket item. It indicated you were probably in construction, farming, or car repair, could likely work with your hands, and might have killed a deer or two. You could not work in an office, wear a tie, or watch *Entourage* or anything like that. You would be ousted before you could say "Dale Earnhardt, seven-time Winston Cup champion."

Killing a deer *might* buy you some points, but it depended on where, when, how, and the circumstances surrounding the kill. For example, if the pull on your compound bow was less than eighty pounds, you were disqualified. You were a sissy.

Fourth, an essential aspect of being accepted on the benches was your personal vehicle. Remember, we were in an area where our country's name was actually pronounced 'Murica—not in the fake Hollywood way. Your vehicle had better be made in the contiguous forty-eight states or at least bear the name of an American automobile maker.

There were no "Tie-otas" or "High-un-days" sitting in the parking lot unless it was a woman or an out-of-towner. If one found himself in a foreign vehicle, the best course of action was to claim you were fixing it for someone else.

"Aw, hell. My cousin Terry's coworker drives this thing. The drive shaft is busted, and I'm a-fixin' it."

"Oh yeah, well, what's your Browning 12-gauge doing in the backseat?"

Cassville men always backed into their parking spot too. No self-respecting man on our benches simply pulled into the lot—they made a huge production out of it. Whether it was a busted 1993 Ford Ranger or the nicest GMC Yukon in the county, we reversed into the spot and gave the engine one last rev before the keys came out of the ignition.

If someone purchased a new vehicle, this was a major event. Every man on the bench popped up and affixed grandiose statements upon the new purchase until one man stepped to the plate and said, "Pop the hood, boy!"

Once the hood was popped, the men gathered around to critique the innards of the new vehicle. This was a time-honored southern tradition, as important as college football, the Daytona 500, and a weekly visit to Waffle House. Cigarettes were lit and fingers pointed as opinions and ultimatums flew.

"I see y'all got 4.6 liter. A boy at work's gotta 5.4 liter, probably a little faster."

"Be sure you got them titanium alloy metric bolts. Them other ones ain't worth a flip now."

"What's the idling RPMs? I hear this model runs hot…"

"I bet you won't git on it!"

Fifth, numerous topics were touched upon out there—from construction and car repair, politics, the weather, the Atlanta Braves, and women. Now, anybody from anywhere could discuss these topics. What differentiated the men on the benches from everyone else was *how* they talked about it. Hyperbole, colloquialisms, and swearing were a must.

"Hell, if that damn Obama keeps raisin' taxes, I'm paddlin' my ass to Cuba!"

Everyone nodded in agreement. The reaction would be far different if you said, "This tax increase proposed by the Obama administration is disconcerting. I fear that a move to another country may be on the horizon. I will Skype with my accountant in the Caymans forthwith."

When people from out of town needed directions, these men were the Google Maps of the 1990s. The only difference was the vernacular and no "recalculating." I often pitied the poor Yankees who were lost and pulled into our parking lot to ask the men how to get to Rome.

"Aw, hell, just go down here to the four lane, take a left at that rock wall, and go down yonder a piece, and the Rome Highway is down there," said Will.

"Naw, that ain't the best way," said Malcolm. "Go down here and get on the four lane, take a left down by the pasture at Griffin Road, go down at Kingston, and hang a right at that trailer with the broke-down Dodge in the front yard."

These poor people from Ohio, Pennsylvania, and Michigan would just look dumbfounded as the men would proceed to argue about how to find a town twenty minutes away. Their eyes would glaze over as Will and Malcolm would carry on.

"It takes three less minutes—me and Margie done drove over there that way to see her brother and ate at the Red Lobster. They got them cheese biscuits."

"Naw, they put in the Walmart out yonder, and it added seven minutes to my drive. I ain't wasting my gas. That back road is faster, and they got that statuary out there, and I need to get daddy a new headstone."

I would just walk over and tell them, "You just can't get there from here."

"Recalculating. Recalculating…"

Sixth, while the rest of the country was going to pieces over Big Tobacco in the '90s, Cassville basically went in the opposite direction. I thought our cigarette and smokeless tobacco sales actually *increased*. (In other words, ain't nobody salutin' the surgeon general in the 30123.)

This could not be more true on those benches. Those guys were walking, talking tobacco advertisements. Nothing put the exclamation point on a diatribe about installing sprinkler pipe in Rocky Face, Georgia, like a huge drag from a Marlboro Red. Nothing conveyed disgust over the Department of Transportation's Draconian policies than spitting a stream of Skoal Long Cut with a hand wipe and a headshake.

You had to hold the cigarette between your lips for long amounts of time without squinting. Failing to do this would show them you were not a real man. You also must have smoked long enough to "try and quit" but must have failed miserably because of the aforementioned divorces and "growed" children.

Having a Zippo was a huge plus, and no knockoff crap was allowed—cheap cigarettes were for white trash, teenagers, and scumbags blowing their welfare checks.

Packing the cigarettes prior to opening them was a dramatization that each man performed before he could light up. Taking a deep breath and smashing the pack into his palm, turning it a few times while making at least one comment about the contents of his rain gauge, three-quarter-inch lag bolts, or somebody's new truck at work.

An overall-clad World War II veteran named Joe would slam his Marlboros into his giant hands so hard that I expected the pack to explode everywhere, but they never did.

"Them things don't smoke right if I don't pack 'em," he would say. It sounded like the cigarettes were children who needed to be threatened with a whuppin' before they could come out to play. He would pull out the newly disciplined cigarette, now beaten into perfect submission, and light it up. The smoke would waft over his wrinkled face, and I would laugh quietly to myself—you just did not laugh in the face of a man who took a shotgun blast from his ex-wife and rescued downed pilots in the Atlantic Ocean in 1943.

Plus, and most importantly, the large majority of these men were packing heat. Whether it be a .22 Derringer, a .38 Special or a .380 strapped to their ankle, the men on the benches of Cass Grocery were ready for trouble. People often wondered why we were never robbed. It was no secret, really. A robber foolish enough to try us would be cut down in a hail of gunfire at 1810 Cassville Road.

This was the place where the "Cassville Seventh Amendment" was created. That is when you shoot a lowlife, criminal or useless person and shut the hell up about it. In other words, some people needed to be killed and these men would be happy to oblige.

So, if you are ever in Cassville, or any small town, and you see a group of men hanging around in front of a store, stop by. Stand around and listen. Observe them in all their glory. If you get a chance, don a flannel shirt, light a cigarette, and repeat the following: "By God, it's hotter than four hells out here. I was Bush Hoggin' my field and ran out of cigarettes. Must've left my other pack at the VFW bar last night."

Solid gold.

CHAPTER 4

Cassville Traffic Shows Us No "Mercey"

FOR YEARS, CASSVILLE HAD ABSOLUTELY no traffic lights. In fact, the road I grew up on was not fully paved until I was in tenth grade. We had that bootleg gravel, Sakrete and dirt mix, for years, rendering car washes useless and causing some nasty scrapes when Matt and I would fly downhill on our bikes, shooting down imaginary MiGs and "breaking hard left."

I'm not sure who I was, Maverick or Ice Man, but I loved to say that "the plaque for the alternates is in the ladies' room" after blowing Russians out the sky. I thoroughly enjoyed watching them crash and burn in Two Run Creek and then celebrating with a milkshake at Neen's.

The road that ran in front of the store, Cassville Road, was paved with actual asphalt. It might have had a thousand potholes, but the citizens living on its frontage enjoyed the perks of pavement. One of the perks of pavement was the speed limit. This stretch of road was like a racetrack. The speed limit was thirty-five miles per hour, but it was hardly acknowledged. There were no stop signs, no traffic, no yields, and no police officers, so Cassville natives could travel at warp speed at all times.

There were good reasons to be in a hurry up there. You did *not* want to miss the Evening Cash 3 drawing, did you? There was one sign close to the store indicating that a sharp curve was ahead, but it did not seem to slow anyone down.

Further, somebody spray-painted "No Mercey" on the sign in 1994, so I guessed the artist was telling us to put the hammer down. When I left Cassville for Athens in 1999, that sign was still there, a glowing sentiment to the local education system.

For years, the hammer stayed down. Guys in Camaros, fresh off the racks and the removal of the muffler, would fly by the store. (For those who are unaware, taking the muffler off makes the car louder, plus it's cheaper than Flowmasters.) The T-tops removed, the IROC-Z lettering glistening in the sun, mullet flying like a flag in the wind, Foreigner and/or Journey blaring out of the Kenwood...nothing punctuated going seventy-five in a thirty-five like "Hot Blooded" or "Only the Young."

Many guys would slide the transmission into neutral, revving their engines and shifting back into drive as they passed the parking lot. This was a Cassville man's way of saying, "What it is, jive turkey?" We would always throw up our hands and yell at them. We didn't care that they drove like a bat out of hell. It burned gas faster, and they would come back and buy it from us.

In the early twenty-first century, I guess the county had received enough complaints about the speed on Cassville Road to do something about it. Contrary to my personal opinion, no "death quota" had been reached. I'd always felt that the Department of Transportation waited until two or three tragic accidents occurred before traffic control was considered. However, as fast as people traveled on Cassville Road, I did not remember any serious accidents. I did remember one man got his bumper knocked off turning left off Cass-White Road, and the bumper skidded down the road and past me with sparks flying—and into the fence next to the store. The guys on the benches went crazy. I thought one of them took it home.

That particular intersection was the focus of the DOT and the new traffic-control device. Since there was already a stop sign on Cass-White and Jo-Ree Roads (which both intersected Cassville Road directly across from one another), they decided to affix two new, shiny red octagons on Cassville Road, making it a four-way stop. Just for good measure, they also added a blinking red light.

This process took about three weeks to complete, and it was all the rage in Cassville.

"There's our damn tax money at work!" exclaimed the men on the benches.

They noted that it required seventeen men to put a stop sign in the ground and at least forty-seven to get that red light up. I think between them all, those workers smoked 13,278 cigarettes, took 327 breaks, and made 2,908 Nextel two-way calls during that time. Money well spent.

This new addition was unveiled, and it did not take long for the problems to arise. There were more wrecks in two weeks than we had seen in fifteen years up there. People running the stop signs, rear-ending each other, and misunderstanding what the blinking lights meant. The amount of quarter panels, taillights, and headlights that met their shattering end at that intersection was immeasurable.

Every time an accident would happen, the peanut gallery on the benches would yell, "Godamighty! The county done it again!" A crowd would accumulate on Cassville Road, opinions would fly, and eventually the entire episode would be blamed on the county.

One stop sign was hit by a woman in a van backing out of the parking lot at the store, shattering her back glass and bending the stop sign to a ninety-degree angle. Mischievous pedestrians would damage them at night with rocks, bats, and graffiti.

Before it was just people driving fast—now it was fender benders and rubbernecking. Lots of head shaking at church on Sunday about the danger now plaguing Cassville. All of this could have been prevented if the DOT had just left us to our own devices. In fact, I could only think of five worse ideas than this four-way stop:

1) Referring to Lonnie Smith, Jane Fonda, or Kent Hrbek without disgust in your voice
2) Not claiming to be at least 1/32 Charkee (Cherokee). This was a dead giveaway that you were not from Cassville, because we were *all* part Cherokee.
3) Admitting you do not have a rain gauge, a commemorative Elvis plate for three easy installments of $9.99, or a tool box on your truck
4) Refer to Gatlinburg as "too redneck."
5) Asking to borrow someone else's Bush Hog

One day after the four-way stop was installed, I was standing out front with Larry, one of our oldest and most loyal customers. Larry had lived in Cassville for the majority of his seventy-six years and had seen it all. He came up to the store every day and hung around for hours, keeping us entertained and just generally overseeing everything. People called him "the mayor of Cassville."

After my grandfathers passed away, he more or less took their place in my life. The first time I met him, he grinned at me and said, "Boy, you'd rather rub sand in a lion's ass than to mess with me." Our greeting to each other was a middle finger, and if I ever shot him a bird first, he would grumble, "You little shitass, you." I knew we were meant for each other.

If there was a model citizen for the benches of Cass Grocery, Larry was it. He was the standard by which everyone was measured—he always wore work boots, flannel, and a mesh-back cap that advertised some sort of concrete business, auto repair shop, or plumbing company. His youth was full of wild stories about fistfights, mischief, and mayhem.

Most of his stories started with these words: "This one time, me, the Edwards boys, and Fain Jordan was fightin' a bunch of people over in Kingston…" He would say it in a voice that sounded like a cross between Clint Eastwood, Sam Elliott, and Billy Bob Thornton.

At the age of sixteen, he served in the navy during the Second World War. His mother helped him lie about his age because, as he said, "She was worried that I'd be killed by the crowd I was runnin' with back then." Seriously, his mother helped him volunteer for military service because she was afraid he would be killed in Bartow County anyway. That was quite epic, if you asked me.

He owned a backhoe that he used to dig the holes for practically every septic tank and deceased horse north of Macon, Georgia. Larry's beady eyes and face—weathered from years of working in the sun and some hard living that he'd left behind years before—his gravelly voice, and general outward toughness made him the quintessential man to us.

A drunk driver missed the turn at Cass-White Road and smashed into our store one summer night in 1994. I will never forget it because Mr. Gwin, one of our best customers, was coming home from a business trip and was the first person to see the wreckage. He drove to our house and we all went up there together to assess the damage. It was like a bad dream. Dad was beside himself with anger and worry.

The entire grocery section was destroyed. A brand new shipment of ammonia had just been delivered, so the smell was unbearable. As we started to pick up the pieces of our family business at first light, a distinct sound rumbled in the distance. Larry's home was nearby and I could see his backhoe coming up Cassville Road toward the store.

He stopped in front of the parking lot and motioned for Dad. After a short discussion, Dad told us to move out of the way as Larry cleaned the entire disaster and hauled it off to the landfill. Larry finished a job in three hours that would have taken us an entire day and night. He refused payment for months and did not want recognition.

"Y'all would the same for me," Larry said. He was family, honestly. He was a pallbearer for Mr. Gus, RB and my grandfather. I guess Larry was right, we would have done anything for him.

Larry had certain quirks that made him predictably awesome. He always had a carpenter's pencil, a pair of pliers, and an extendable wooden ruler in the pocket of his pants or shirt. He did not suffer fools, smart alecks, kids with pants "hangin' halfway down their ass," self-righteousness, or people who caused us trouble. These types of people avoided Larry because he would not allow them the time of day and did not hide his disdain for them. This attitude endeared him to us even further.

One particular day, Larry and I were watching the cars go by, talking about the Braves and how last night's game turned out. (Larry had a love/hate relationship with them, and we bet on every game. If the Braves won, he bought me a Mountain Dew. If they lost, I had to buy him a pack of hot peanuts.) I noticed Larry looking at the four-way stop intently, and I could see his wheels turning.

Larry chewed tobacco constantly, and he was just standing there, working the wad in his mouth and looking at the traffic. At the stop signs, there were a total of five cars waiting their turn to go, with maybe twelve people total sitting in them. Larry got this disgusted look on his face, shook his head, and spit on the ground. He wiped his mouth, looked at me with his squinty eyes, and said, "Damn, where'd all these people come from?"

(I don't know, Larry. I truly don't know. The urban sprawl shows us "No Mercey." God bless us.)

CHAPTER 5

Wild Onions and Rabbit Tobacco Are the Keys to Happiness

As with many close-knit Southern families, my people lived within walking distance of one another. Mom's family lived in Anderson, South Carolina and most of them lived within five miles of one another. Peepaw and Meemaw raised Mom and my uncles in a small house on Avondale Road about ten minutes outside of downtown Anderson. They worked hard for every penny and never complained about anything. If they lived in Cassville, they would have fit right in.

The majority of Dad's family lived in Cassville on Kimsey Circle, named after my great-grandfather, Julius David Kimsey. "Daddy Kim," as he was known to us, was the son of a blacksmith and one of the kindest people in the world. He was rarely seen without a smile on his face.

He worked in at the EZ Mills factory in Cartersville and had more friends than anyone could count. As Larry once told me, "he was the best of us all." If somebody in Cassville was in need, Daddy Kim was usually one of the first people to offer his support. Whether it be food during the Depression, money to get through the week or borrowing his tractor, Daddy Kim went out of his way to help anyone.

He was married to Lucille Shinall Kimsey, known as "Mama Kim" or "Aunt Cille" to the younger generation. She was a short, feisty woman that never missed church and always voted Democrat. I once tried to convince her that she should rethink her position when Bill Clinton was up for re-election.

"Herbert Hoover caused the Depression, boy. He was a Republican. I ain't *never* votin' for another Republican." Mama Kim had a way with words. Slick Willie got at least one vote in Cassville.

Reconnoitering was Mama Kim's specialty. Nothing happened on Kimsey Circle without her knowledge or approval. She knew every inch of that ground because she "used to sneak off and smoke rabbit tobacco there" when she was a teenager. Every movement registered on Mama Kim's personal radar: cars leaving driveways, people walking down the street and especially anything the grandchildren were doing. She used to threaten me with a spatula when I passed by her house too fast on Matt's motorcycle. I did it on purpose just to rile her up.

Our phone rang one winter afternoon and Mom answered. It was Mama Kim with a report.

"Susan, I was washing off some butter beans on the porch just now and there is a rooster on top of y'all's van. You know Joe will tear that thing to pieces if he finds it."

Mom darted outside to scare the rooster away. Now, Mama Kim saw every movement in our little universe, but her eyesight was worse than a blindfolded mole at midnight. Climbing the ladder of that Chevy van, Mom found my brother strutting around like a fool. We never told Mama Kim because she would have chastised us all for letting him up there.

Daddy Kim passed away in 1982 and Mama Kim lived alone in their old house. Up the hill from her, separated by a pine thicket, was our house and Neen's trailer. My grandfather, W.L. Stephens, bought that trailer in 1984 and they lived comfortably in their modular existence until his death in 1989. Granddaddy's death was disheartening for all of us, especially Dad.

Granddaddy was the quintessential tough guy, the product of a hardscrabble life that defined the South in those days. He joined the Marines out of high school in 1949. He was a blue collar man that rarely complained, compromised or put up with people's foolishness. Larry was good friends with him and told me, "W.L. wasn't the kind of man you wanted to piss off." Dad recalled a day in the Smoky Mountains that let me know what kind of man my Granddaddy was.

He took Neen, Aunt Melinda and Dad up to Gatlinburg for a weekend in the mid-1960s. They were driving on a lonely mountain road when Granddaddy noticed a pickup truck with three men following their car very closely. He glanced in the rearview mirror a number of times and Dad could feel an uneasy tension in the car.

After a couple of miles and making every turn with him, Granddaddy was not waiting around to find out if they wanted trouble. He pulled over in an empty gravel lot and sure enough, the truck did the same. Granddaddy sighed and glared in the rearview mirror one last time.

"Y'all stay put," Granddaddy told everyone in the car. There was a wave of calm on his face, as if he knew exactly what to do. He took his .38 pistol out of the glove box and marched back to the truck without hesitation. The men in the truck did not have time to react.

"I don't know what y'all are planning to do, but I'll tell you one thing, I will kill all three of you right now and not lose a wink of sleep over it. Put this truck in gear and get outta here. Now."

The men did not say a word, not even a denial. Gravel flew everywhere as the would-be criminals lost their nerve and took off down the highway. Granddaddy calmly walked back to the car, stored the pistol and drove off as if nothing happened.

I used to watch *Austin City Limits* with him in their living room. We sat by each other in church while he drew clowns on the bulletin to make me laugh. He would eat an entire half-gallon of cherry vanilla ice cream in his recliner while I admired his Marine Corps tattoos. He made me promise not to ever get one, though.

Neen never remarried and I was her de facto roommate for ten years. If I was ever in trouble, I always ran to Neen, who would spoil me with cookies, milkshakes and homemade vanilla ice cream. Nothing was ever my fault. Even though Dad was her son, she always took my side and would stay mad at him for days.

Beyond feeding me all the fattening goodness I wanted, Neen let me run wild all over the family acreage. We used to get in Two Run Creek and find periwinkles together. I would hunt squirrels and snakes all around the pond behind her trailer. There were no ordinances or concerns about such activity and I became a crack shot with my .22 Marlin. Gunfire on Kimsey Circle drew as much attention as a dog barking back in those days.

We had a pasture full of clover and a dirt path around it that Mama Kim called "The Cotton Patch Road." There was a cove in the pasture where we would shoot skeet and sight in rifles on weekends. It was common to see deer, turkeys, and coyotes roaming around the pasture at all hours of the day. Queen Anne's Lace and maypops bordered the path all the way to the big hill that separated our property from the farmer across the way.

That hill was mysterious, especially at dusk. Not only was it covered in dense vegetation that blocked the sunlight, it was the site of a skirmish during Sherman's March to the Sea in 1864. The Confederate defenders and Union attackers clashed in trenches at the top of the hill and several men lost their lives. There was an eerie feeling every time I went up there alone, the silence of the birds was a telltale sign that something was amiss. I swear I could see the shadows move up there.

Our house was shrouded by pines, dogwoods, one giant oak tree and a plum tree. Matt and I used those trees for climbing, hiding and as bases during our many aggressive Wiffle ball games. Those games caused several black eyes and bloody noses, but we lived to tell about it. A home run was awarded to anyone who could smack that ball over the power lines that ran across the front yard. I still have a scar from catching a rock in my calf as I slid into second base on Sunday afternoon.

That plum tree was also the source of fear, as that was the tree that bore the dreaded "switches" Dad used when we were misbehaving. It was not very often, but when we stepped out of line, Dad was not in the business of empty threats. Discipline came swift and we learned to walk the straight and narrow quickly. Mom was always the salve for our wounds, but she knew when we needed to learn our lesson. There were no "time outs" on Kimsey Circle.

Matt and I must have worn out thirty bicycles, fifty fishing rods and one hundred basketballs during those years. We rarely saw the inside of our house in the daylight. Our jeans were always torn, our knees were always scraped and our shirts stayed filthy from playing in the dirt. I cannot count the stalks of poke sallet that we destroyed with our four-wheeler. Poor Mom endured a never ending pile of laundry, but she never complained. I guess she never got tired of our dirt bike racing, tree house building and wild onion fights.

A wild onion fight broke out at least once a week at our house. These pesky plants grew everywhere on our property and they were the perfect weapon. If you grabbed the leaves close to the bulb and pulled carefully, the plant would come out of ground with a large clod of red clay attached. Throwing this missile and hitting Matt in the chest was one of my favorite pastimes. Matt used guerilla tactics on me, often materializing from behind trees or Mama Kim's bushes.

The road itself was a bumpy mix of dirt, gravel, broken asphalt and springs of weeds growing out of old cracks. For years, it was unmarked and simply known as Rural Route 3 to mail carriers. There were no lanes, as there was only room for one vehicle at a time. When the county finally paved the road in 1997, it was sad because the Cassville Skateboard Club (Membership: Matt and I) initiation was to skate down the hill at maximum speed without hitting a pothole and wiping out.

Our neighbors to the north lived in two rows of houses on either side of the road. Most of them had outside dogs, a satellite dish, a slew of children and at least one inoperable vehicle in the front yard. It was a friendly neighborhood and most everyone got along, unless the dogs got into a scrape or somebody got drunk and decided to rebuild their Mustang engine at 3:37 a.m.

It was a simple, happy existence that I would not trade for anything in the world.

CHAPTER 6

The Stray Cat Strut and Cassville's Own Episode of *Cheaters*

MY APARTMENT IN NEW YORK City was located at the intersection of West Seventy-Ninth Street and Amsterdam Avenue, right between the Westside Highway and Central Park. This corner was extremely busy most of the time, as Seventy-Ninth was one of the few thoroughfares in the Park, so everyone needing to cross from the Upper East and Upper West Sides careened up and down the hill by my apartment every day.

There was a great deli right there called Amsterdam Gourmet—a place where you could get an excellent Italian sub, European chocolates, or homemade baklava and rugelach. The family of Jordanian immigrants that operated the deli were obsessed with my accent and always asked me the same question: "Hey, buddy? Buddy? It's hot in Georgia, no?" There was never a moment in Amsterdam Gourmet where a soccer game was not on the television.

(Speaking of soccer, I am not certain that Cassville folks are aware that soccer is a sanctioned sport. If it is not football, baseball, NASCAR or firearm involved, I guarantee you that Cassville televisions are not tuned in. You can count me in with that crowd.)

When I was visiting Ireland, I watched, in a bar in Dublin, Manchester United play Arsenal. I thought a town full of drunken soccer hooligans would definitely get me fired up about this game.

Wrong. The three-hour marathon game ended in a 0–0 tie. Observing the Irish crowd going ballistic over the anemia that was this soccer match, I was simply confounded. In essence, we had just watched a bunch of European and African males run twenty miles apiece—an exercise in pointlessness that could have been accomplished in a camping chair on the sidewalk at the end of the New York Marathon.

All I had to show for my efforts was a hangover from too much Guinness, a bill for below-average bangers and mash, and a three-page write-up the next morning in the *Irish Daily Star* about how each team *almost* scored. In fact, if I made a list of "most boring things on planet Earth," watching a 0–0 soccer match would fall somewhere between a discussion about super-unleaded and unleaded-plus gasoline and getting a scented candle for your birthday.

My intersection in New York was a cacophony of taxicabs, blaring horns, buses making the stop on the northeast corner, delivery trucks trying to keep schedules, and New Jersey commuters attempting warp speed as they headed back to the Lincoln Tunnel. (Not to mention, New York is a pedestrian friendly town. So, add ambulatory humans and their decision-making processes to this mass of moving parts, and you have the recipe for disaster.)

In my three years there, I never saw one accident. Nary a pedestrian was struck by a wayward bus or cab. Nobody was ever pulled over for speeding, running the red light, or weaving through traffic like a schizophrenic squirrel trying to get away from a dog. The only time this intersection was backed up was the bimonthly street fair, the Macy's Thanksgiving Parade, and the day Obama spoke at the Natural History Museum.

The president lost a few supporters that day, especially in my building. The Secret Service would not let us leave our building until the president's motorcade passed by at eight, but it was running late. People had reservations at restaurants, concerts to attend, and tickets to movies and Broadway shows that were being missed.

The elderly Mrs. Goldberg pitched such a fit that the agents finally let her leave—apparently Jewish guilt can overcome federal protocols to protect the leader of the free world.

Intersections like this were nonexistent in Cassville. The number of cars that passed by my apartment in New York in thirty minutes probably exceeded the number of cars that passed by Cass Grocery in a full day. There were times that I could have lain down on Cassville Road and taken a nap without disturbance. It picked up when school let out or when it was quitting time for the nine-to-five people, but it paled in comparison to Seventy-Ninth Street.

Despite the modest number of people, the intersection of Cass-White Road and Cassville Road was chock full of the drama, controversy, comedy, and mischievous activity that made Cassville so special. This dusty corner of the universe completely destroyed Seventy-Ninth Street in this regard.

I was baptized into the church of Cassville Road drama early on.

My uncle Mike, who worked with us for several years, found a stray cat wandering out there one day while we were talking in a group. He was an animal lover, so his inclination was to pick it up and pet it. We warned him to leave it alone; stray animals in Cassville were no joke. They almost always bit and probably had diseases only found in the hinterlands of New Guinea. I would see them at the Dumpster, and I swore those cats would talk to each other. Evil little minions, they were.

He placed the cat on his arm and started rubbing its back and patting its head. The cat's fur smelled like the wrath of God, but my uncle hardly seemed to notice. Larry was telling a story about a brawl when he was in the navy, and we all focused on him. We loved Larry's stories about his escapades in the 1940s and how lawless it used to be.

About a minute went by, and we heard "Awwww, damn!"

The cat, rather than bite his hand or claw him, sprayed diarrhea all over my uncle's forearm. He grabbed the cat by the scruff of the neck and wrung his arm to remove the foul-smelling excrement. We all scattered, and Mike spun around and threw the cat like a discus across the street. It landed on its feet and ran into the woods, undoubtedly headed to the Dumpster to warn the others. Larry never finished his story but never failed to tell people about Mike's pet cat every day for about two years.

Mike was famous for his erratic driving. The county Dumpster was on Cedar Creek Road and twice a week, Mike would haul off a stinking pile of garbage from the store in the back of Dad's Chevy truck. We would take all the bags, boxes and empty bottles across the street, where the truck was parked, and fill the bed up. Mike would make the U-turn off Mrs. Allen's lot and head north. Most of the time, he would come and go without issue.

Other times, he would pull one of his stunts and somebody paid the price. One quiet Tuesday afternoon, my car was victimized. I parked behind Dad every day without fail, just as any other worker up there would do. Dad ordered us to haul off the trash and we loaded the truck down for Mike to take to the Dumpster.

When I say it was a quiet Tuesday afternoon, I mean dead silence. The wind was not blowing. Birds were not chirping. You could have marched an entire Marine battalion down Cassville Road without worry. It was one of those summer days that was so hot and humid that it felt like breathing with a dirty dishrag on your face.

Mike hopped in the truck and inexplicably, shifted into reverse and backed that Chevy into my car. My hood made that awful sound as the steel bed scraped over the top and removed all of the paint.

"Aw dang," I muttered. I knew Dad would blow a fuse.

"Mike! What the hell?!?"

"I'm sorry Dave, I thought I needed to back up. I didn't have room, I..."

"No room! Mike, you got half of Cassville to turn this truck around!"

He drove the truck off the road and into a creek about a year later. Mike also knocked the head off of a German Shepherd coming home from the Dumpster. He parked and made a beeline for the walk-in cooler, as if nothing happened. I saw Dad's headlight dangling with bloody fur stuck in the grill and had no choice but to let Dad know. He jerked the door of the cooler open.

"Mike! Get out here!"

"Yeah, Dave? What can I do for you?"

"What did you do to my truck?!?"

"It ain't my fault. That dog walked out in front of me."

I had to get the headless carcass off Cassville Road and toss it into the woods before anyone saw it. We all loved Mike. He used to think he was Sonny Crockett and wore linen suits around town during the 1980s. He even carried a gun. God help us.

Stay Away from Misty

I was outside pumping gas and checking oil often, so I had a front-row seat when things got out of hand. In the summer of 1995, I was putting ten dollars of gas in an old Buick, one of the models where the gas line was behind the license plate in the back. It was about 6:30 a.m., and I was half-asleep when a beat-up Chevy van pulled to a stop at the intersection.

On the side of this van was an airbrushed mural of a horse leaping over a canyon with lightning striking in the background. The running board was scraping the asphalt. A Hefty bag served as one of the back windows, and primer gray along with thirty-seven shades of brown were the colors of this rattletrap. *Rattletrap* was one of my favorite words used by Neen. Any vehicle that was in disrepair or made too much noise was awarded this nickname. "Here come them Ray people in that rattletrap they got, ugh."

I heard yelling coming from the open windows. A skinny man in a cutoff shirt was driving, and his much-larger female passenger (field dressing around 265 pounds) were having a heated argument. It was actually less of an argument and more of her screaming at him while he just sat there and took his verbal beating.

"I done *told* you to stay away from Misty, that little whore! But oh no! You just can't help yourself, Dwayne! You mother—"

"But, baby, it didn't mean nothin!"

My half-asleep state had now graduated to fully awake. Bonnie, the gas customer, had stuck her head out of her window to observe the animals in their natural habitat. As Dwayne tried to take the turn toward Adairsville on Cassville Road, his girlfriend cocked her right arm and landed a jab to his right jaw. The force of the blow caused Dwayne to lose his grip on the steering wheel, but his foot did not leave the gas pedal. The van smashed into a telephone pole, and the hood accordioned up to the windshield.

The girlfriend jumped out and circled around, dragged Dwayne out of the driver's seat, and continued to pummel him. She was uttering profanity that would have to remain in the silent annals of history. I could not help but notice she was still in her nightgown and house shoes, which flew off as she kicked him on the ground. I stared as the fight ended with Dwayne finally kicking the girl's legs out from under her. She hit the pavement with a thud and then sat up, sobbing. The van was smoking up the entire intersection with exhaust because it was still running, I had mistakenly pumped $13.76 into Bonnie's car, and a crowd of men had gathered out front, laughing hysterically and catcalling.

"You better run, boy!"

"Dwayne, you oughta move to Sugar Valley with your mama!" screamed Harold, one of our regulars.

I told Bonnie of my mistake, and she gladly paid. "Hey, that was worth $3.76. Made my day!" Dwayne helped his girl up, and they leaned against the abandoned building across the street. After being punched, kicked, called every name in the book, and destroying his van, Dwayne hugged her. They crossed the street and bought some coffee and biscuits from us.

That never happened on Seventy-Ninth Street.

BIKERS BEWARE

In the mid-1990s, a new tradition began to take place in Cassville every spring. The annual Bicycle Ride across Georgia, better known as BRAG, would meander its way into Bartow County and pass right by our store on a Saturday. BRAG was a gathering of men and women, mostly from suburban Atlanta, who would strap on their helmets and pedal their $2,000 road bikes down the rural pathways of the Peach State. The concept was interesting, but I never understood the fun of riding a bike that did not have crushed Coke cans between the tires and wheel wells.

Dad, being the rural entrepreneur he was, moved the hot dogs and barbecue outside on this day. Coolers full of Gatorade, Powerade, Coca-Cola, and Mountain Dew were wheeled out into the parking lot. Mom made poster-board signs directing these road warriors to fuel their bodies with our food and drink. The intersection would look like an aquarium full of tetras swimming in all directions as fast as possible. Except, these were dorky white people who wore ill-fitting tights and probably sold insurance on one of the ten thousand "Peachtree" roads in Atlanta.

Early in the day, it was gangbusters. The whole family had to work. Neen and Mom served the food, Matt and I stocked the coolers, and Dad took the money. It was quite the little enterprise for about four hours.

As the day wore on, the bikers were less concerned with buying sustenance and more worried about using our bathroom. Neen would take off, so as to not miss her soap operas, saying, "Damn these people—the *Young and the Restless* waits for no man." Dad would get annoyed with the constant use of our free toilet and go home with Mom, leaving Matt and I to our own devices.

This was probably not unique to Cassville, but there was one thing that nobody in Cassville could abide—condescension. Since many of these people came from affluent areas, there was an air of superiority about them that did not sit well with us. Like many Atlantans, they did not have a southern accent or southern mannerisms. Eventually, I told them the bathroom was out of order. That was when the smart-aleck comments came out.

"You guys don't have running water here?"

"Just let me use it. You can fix it later. You people are handy anyway."

"Is there an outhouse?"

Matt definitely hated this attitude, and one year he decided enough was enough. If there was one thing I could say for my brother, he was not afraid to do anything for a laugh or to prove a point.

Taking matters into his own hands, he went back to the hardware and grabbed a garden hoe. He removed his T-shirt and tied it around his head like a bootleg turban. He rolled up one pant leg and took off one shoe.

As the bikers rode by, he walked toward them with a fake limp, dragging the hoe behind him and letting sparks fly off the asphalt. He moaned loudly and looked up at them with one closed eye and drool on his lip. I could see the pity on their faces as my mischievous brother moved closer.

"Poor kid."

"Wow, they really are inbred."

"I hope his parents are around."

Just as Matt moved near the constant stream of bikers and the sympathy was at its peak, Matt sprang to life and screamed bloody murder, wielding the garden hoe. He darted toward a line of bikers, all of them swerving and pedaling as fast as they could. He ran in circles, swinging wildly and making the bikers look like a herd of wildebeests running from a pride of lions.

The smart-aleck comments and constant requests to use the bathroom completely stopped because none of the bikers would come near us. My brother wandered the road all day long, patrolling for wayward bikers who dared to cross his path. The men on the benches howled with delight as Matt singlehandedly changed the BRAG route forever.

They never came through Cassville again.

CHAPTER 7

Smith & Wesson is Not a Law Firm

I WAS PAID THE ULTIMATE compliment last year. A friend of mine from Cassville sent a message to me on Facebook asking about how I enjoyed my legal career. After discussing my daily duties, she replied, "I was shocked to know you became a lawyer. Not because it's hard, but because every lawyer I know is a whiny, wimpy, lying jerk, and none of those words describe you at all."

Totally flattered, I thanked her. Sadly, I cannot disagree with her indictment of my profession, as I see many lawyers every day who fit that bill. The chances of the average person running into a lawyer that is a "whiny, wimpy, lying jerk" increase every day, as law schools keep churning them out left and right to a world with limited jobs, where the premium shifts from service to the client over to "I gotta get mine."

I've often asked myself, after meeting one of these types, "This guy passed the same bar I did?" Yep, he sure as hell did. So I see it as my duty to prove to the world that some of us still have decorum, still care about our fellow man, and understood our oath to mean more than just a license to don silk stockings and ride the elevator of self-importance.

Frankly, every profession, every religion, race, and creed has extreme negative sides.

I had my first encounter with a Hare Krishna member during my first year in New York. He started handing me trinkets and a card that said "Peace" with an illustration of Krishna, and he blessed me over and over, telling me that he prayed for peace in my life, blah blah blah. I say "blah blah blah" because he immediately asked for a donation, and I replied that I only had a credit card, which was true. His smile disappeared, he jerked his trinkets out of my hand, and darted away quickly, ready to con the next person.

I tried to let it go, but I could not. In New York, I learned that confrontation was warranted at a moment like this. You know why I was mad? I was listening to a live version of "Wish You Were Here" by Pink Floyd, enjoying it immensely, when this little rip-off artist accosted me. I said, "Don't interrupt David Gilmour ever again." Like I said, some things just cannot be ignored. Plus, they wore Tennessee-orange robes, so they automatically joined my shit list just by existing.

There were so many types of people in New York, and I became immune to the "different" folks who called it home. A guy wearing an orange Mohawk and a tattoo on his face? Not a second look. I saw a woman walking topless next to Grand Central, wearing nothing but jeans and a cowboy hat. I paid her about as much attention as a pigeon pecking at the horse feed next to Central Park. She actually stopped next to a phone booth and adjusted her hat in her reflection off the glass. Apparently, if you were wearing half of a birthday suit, you wanted to look your best for your eventual jail visit.

I watched a homeless man absolutely "dog cuss" (a great southern term) the padlocked door on the UPS store. I actually stopped for this one, because he was using combinations of foul language that I had never heard in my life, and I thought that maybe God actually could strike him dead. He would start walking away and then would come back and rip into this padlocked door like it had just stolen his iPhone. (Homeless people have iPhones in New York—no kidding.) This procession continued for five minutes until he realized he had more pressing business uptown and walked off for good. As I walked by that door, I swore I almost overheard it talking smack.

Cassville has about 8.4 million less people than New York. If you wear an orange Mohawk, people will probably stare at you. You will probably be accused of being an atheist, or worse, a Democrat. We have precisely five restaurants, and only one that is not located in a truck stop. There are no cabs for hire riding around—you have to call them. Then they show up in a busted 1994 Ford Aerostar, looking half-dead and telling you that they don't go past Fairmount. Pizza is not our thing, and Papa John's refuses to go past Mac Johnson Road, cutting us off almost completely.

Street vendors don't sell pashminas or knockoff Louis Vuitton purses. They sell autographed Dale Earnhardt Jr. helmets out of their front yard. The closest version of Times Square? Exit 296 with its truck stops, three hotels (one condemned), and the adult book store. You can see the lights all the way from Adairsville. You want to run through our Central Park and get a taste of history? There's a patch of grass next to Cass Grocery that you could run around about 2,754 times. It has a monument to Lewis Cass, for whom the town is named.

However, what we lack in nightlife and activity, we make up for with character.

First, we know what WD-40 can do and that its value is second only to duct tape. How many door hinges, engine parts, and bicycle chains did I grease back home? Countless. Plus, you can make an awesome flamethrower with it. God help any fire ants that built a nest in the parking lot at Cass Grocery. We are talking hell-like conditions for these poor insects while my brother and I danced around them like fools. Why burn just one with a magnifying glass? That's inefficient. People in New York probably think it's something you file with your taxes.

Second, we know Briggs & Stratton, Smith & Wesson, and Allis-Chalmers. We know Dean Durham, Shaw Grigsby, and Denny Brauer. People in New York probably think these are all law firms. I cannot count how many Briggs & Stratton spark plugs I sold at the store, and I would run back to the TV because Bill Dance was coming on, and I did not want to miss the bloopers.

Third, we can talk about pouring concrete, installing drywall, working on a car, or hanging shingles for hours. In fact, we can make it into a dramatization. Forget Broadway. Imagine one man in front of Cass Grocery talking to six other men drinking coffee.

"So, there's Lamar. He's got the manifold in his hand. He tells Bobby to put the air filter back in, but Bobby can't find it. They get to fightin'." ("Get to fightin'" is a great southern term.)

The group all looks at each other with an understanding glance. Fighting over an air filter...totally worth it. Some of them grumble about the price of air filters, and there's a sidebar discussion of Advance Auto, AutoZone, and Cass Grocery prices. They all decide they would rather buy from us because they like us, take a sip of coffee, and the story continues.

"So, Bobby goes to lookin'. He can't find the air filter nowhere. Y'all know how dumb he is. All over the shop, he tears up everything, lookin' for this air filter. Sure enough, the damn dog took it, and it was tore up all over the yard. Lamar had to go all the way back to Cartersville [four miles] to get another one."

During this riveting exchange, nobody takes their eyes off the storyteller. They laugh uncontrollably at Lamar's expense, then somebody tells a story about Sheetrock falling off the wall at a job. Like old man river, it never stops.

Fourth, we don't have a homeless problem. Everybody lives somewhere, by God. Since we all claim fifth and sixth cousins and are all 1/32 Cherokee, it's like one big happy family...we just pile into a single-wide on Cedar Creek Road, stick a mailbox in the dirt, and call it home. I knew one family on Mostellar's Mill Road, on the Cassville/Adairsville/Folsom border, that must have had fifty-six people living in their house. How did I know? They all wrote me bad checks and had the same address.

Fifth, we don't have a pile of newspapers influencing our political decisions in Cassville. In New York, there's the *Daily News*, the *Times*, the *Post*, the *Wall Street Journal*, and the *Metro* (and that's just off the top of my head). The Upper West Side is an un-designated area with no real boundaries, yet it has its own weekly newspaper.

The only magazines that anyone ever asked for at Cass Grocery were the latest *Auto Trader* or *Georgia Outdoor News*. We cared more about the biggest buck taken in Early County and what it scored on the Pope & Young (also not a law firm) than what some politician felt about the latest SPLOST proposal.

The 30123 may not have the bright lights, it may not have any restaurants that can get higher than a seventy-three on the health inspection, and we may not be able to get pizza other than DiGiorno from Ingles, but we definitely have a way of life unique to us. I've told New Yorkers, who are in disbelief at the size and quiet nature of my hometown, that we're never bored. Seriously, who would not be entertained by a story about fence staples? Who would not want to watch me burn a cockroach with a flame-thrower fueled by WD-40? Who would not want to see a picture of the biggest bream caught in Polk County?

As for the homeless guy cussing the padlocked door, if he did that in Cassville, he would be dealt with as nonchalantly as on the streets of New York. I could hear them at the store now: "I bet that sumbitch is from Fairmount."

CHAPTER 8

There are no Altercations in Cassville

ONE OF MY PET PEEVES in this life is when people use large words where smaller ones will suffice. An SAT word, if you will. People like Stephen A. Smith on ESPN have made this practice cool for this generation, and I hear people going out of their way to use three- and four-syllable words uselessly to sound more intelligent. In reality, they sound dumber than a cord of hickory sticks.

"Conversate" is my all-time most annoying. I have never understood the angle, to be honest. I cannot see where it is necessary to use this word in the place of one of the simplest one-syllable words in the English language: *talk*. On the subway, I overheard two females who "had conversated" with the teacher of their children about their low grades in math class. Of course, it was not the fault of the child and the teacher was "bullying" the children.

Then came my next all-time most annoying: "She said that my child was failing due to lack of assistance at home. I was like, hell naw. She and I about had an altercation…"

That is *not* an altercation. An altercation is when the cops are involved and they want a police report to sound more professional.

"The suspect and the victim had an altercation over carnal knowledge of the female, Tammy..."

Two idiots duking it out in a school yard, or even better, a seedy trailer park, are not having an "altercation."

Cassville did not have altercations. We had fights. Lots of them. Fighting was part of our pastime, and we enjoyed a great story of fists flying, hair pulling, eye gouging, bones breaking, and pride hurting. Whether it be a wayward insult, a cheating lover, a neighborly quarrel, or drunken tomfoolery, all fights were created equal in Cassville. They were all awesome.

Dad never fought anyone, but his verbal assaults on those who offended him were legendary. He once chased the ice delivery man back into his truck for telling one of our customers to hurry up and move. He once cussed the gas delivery man so badly that even Larry got nervous and went home.

"Hell, I'm outta here. Your daddy's gonna blow a gasket."

One of my personal favorites was a woman who accused my dad of selling cigarettes to her underage son. She walked in the door with a satisfied smirk on her face, holding a receipt. She placed her hands on the counter, took a deep breath, and in her most condescending tone, said, "You and I need to have a serious talk."

"About what?" my dad replied, annoyed. Other customers stopped shopping and turned their attention to the impending brouhaha.

"My sixteen-year-old son bought cigarettes from here. I knew he smelled like smoke, so I went through his pants pockets and found this [holding up the receipt]. It's his check card, and there is no denying it. I have already contacted the police and the DARE officer at his school. You are going to be in a lot of trouble. How can you sell cigarettes to children? What kind of man makes money like that? What do you intend to do to fix this issue?"

Her smirk just widened, like she just won a huge bet.

Dad took the receipt and reviewed it.

"You're a teacher at the elementary school, right?" Dad asked calmly.

"Yeah, so?"

"So I assume you can read. Well, I see two problems. One, this receipt says the purchase was made at 10:31 p.m. on Saturday. I close at 7:00 p.m. Second, and most importantly, you see the name on top of the receipt? It says Cass-White Country Store. See the address? Cass-White Road. This is Cass Grocery, and our address is 1810 Cassville Road."

There was an awkward pause. Her smirk disappeared, her eyes went straight to the floor, and her face turned hot pink. Dad's jaw started throbbing, and his face turned purple. Other customers in the store started backing away, and I motioned for them to run.

The stream of words my dad uttered rivaled the first fifteen minutes of *Full Metal Jacket*. This lady was backing out the door, and Dad followed her to her car. She was bawling and apologizing, but Dad was having none of it. She had tried to embarrass him in front of other people, the unforgivable sin. One of the customers said, "Dave ought to slap her." The guys on the benches were silent, except for Ted.

"That dumbass lady. She's gotta know Dave charges more for Marlboros."

COMMON-LAW MARITAL BLISS

There was a common-law couple who came in the store for years, John and Teresa. A large amount of drama existed between them, and every weekend was a "drunk and disorderly" waiting to happen. He worked in the asphalt-laying business, and she was unemployed, sustaining herself through the day with heavy medication, one Marlboro after the other, and at least a twelve pack of Bud Light before 3:00 p.m.

When he would leave to do "road work," as he said, she would go over to her mother's house, and they would start drinking. Both of them stayed pickled most of the day. Teresa's teeth looked like she ate twelve Oreos and forgot to drink the milk. She might have washed her hair once in 1994. Add to that a hot-pink tank top, no bra, white jean shorts, and bare feet—you had Teresa in a nutshell for the majority of her adult life.

There were rumors about Teresa all over town. One especially famous one was that her father actually pimped her out to men when she was in high school and that they would "conduct business" in the back of a service station in White, Georgia. This man was a character himself, and if this rumor had ever been proven, I would not bat an eye. He always wore a greasy hat and filthy coveralls with some other person's name stitched over the left pocket, and he had these beady eyes that just said "I'm a degenerate piece of crap."

Honestly, I never liked him, because he complained about prices to the point where he would grab each item and say, "This is twelve cents cheaper at Walmart. This is sixteen cents cheaper at Home Depot…"

My response was always the same—"Well, they are open, you old bastard." He came back to us every day without fail.

His daughter, on the other hand, never complained about anything. Maybe having a perpetual buzz made Teresa so agreeable. She took a shine to most men when she was hammered out of her gourd, and the employees of Cass Grocery were no exception—well, everybody other than Dad. She was terrified of him.

You could tell when Teresa was lit up, because it took her twenty minutes to get in the door. She would open the passenger door, get out, and then turn back and talk to her mother in the driver's seat. Yes, the mother was drunk too, but she was a better drunk driver than Teresa, who lost her license after five DUIs in three years, including two wrecks and one totaled Chevrolet Silverado belonging to her man, John.

After finally deciding what they needed, Teresa would mosey in the door. She would narrow her eyes at me or whoever was behind the counter and turn on the charm that only drunken thirty-seven-year-old trailer-park women in hot-pink tank tops could.

"Hey. Heeeeeeey. What y'all dooooooin? Mmmmmmm, mmmmm, y'all look good today. Mama would come in, but she ain't able on account of her gout."

She'd stumble away. A beer-cooler visit must come first, always. (Budweiser owes these people a house with fifty acres for the amount of money they have contributed over the years.)

Funyuns, a Snickers bar, and Swiss Cake Rolls came next—Teresa and her mother needed lunch, of course. After stacking the supplies on the counter, she made another round of shameless passes at us.

"Why don't y'all come on back to the house with me? Y'all don't need to work."

After we shuddered at the thought of entering Teresa's trailer, we rang her up and got her out the door as fast as possible. But not before she decided to buy a box of Oatmeal Creme Pies, headache powders, a loaf of bread, and a two-liter grape Fanta. She was thinking ahead about tomorrow's hangover.

Well, the other rumor about Teresa was that she was presently sleeping with pretty much every low-down, destitute man in Bartow County. To fan the flames, several people saw Teresa in pickup trucks not being driven by John at random times throughout the weeks. If I was a betting man, I wouldn't think Teresa and these men were discussing the county's millage rate over tea and crumpets.

Unfortunately for Teresa, John forgot his wallet one day and sent a coworker to his trailer to retrieve it at their lunch break. He pulled up and used John's key to go in, only to find Teresa and another man on the couch. He grabbed John's wallet and evacuated quicker than my pitching wedge skills after a two-month layoff. John was filled in on the details, and the day went south.

John was one of those guys who didn't wear a shirt unless he was at work. He had a gut the size of a pumpkin and random tattoos of former lovers and children's names on his back, a skull on his left bicep, and a bulldog on his right forearm. He looked like "Hacksaw" Jim Duggan ate a keg of beer and then fell down a flight of stairs. He worked on cars in his spare time and always asked us "Who's winnin' the race?" on Sundays. A sandy-blond mullet and a pencil-thin mustache adorned his noggin. While a decent guy, John was prone to violence, and going to jail was not really a concern for him.

John's son went to school with me and he was a spitting image of his father. I was taking a health insurance form to the office one morning and heard a huge commotion in the principal's office. Chairs were flying and the door swung open as the combatants spilled out into the lobby. "Little John" was shirtless, bloody and telling the administrators how far up their posteriors they could shove their heads. He made eye contact with me.

"Stephens! What's up?!?"

"Nothing. What are you up to?"

"Gettin' thowed outta school! I'll be by the store later, Daddy needs some roofing nails."

The chip off the old block was not a bad kid, he just looked for any reason to punch someone in the face. In Cassville, that was not hard to come by.

Although Teresa was a drunken fool that basically begged men to sleep with her out in the open, she was still common-law married to John. The sanctity of the common-law marriage could not be under assault on Cassville Road, by God. The coworker stopped by and told us the seedy details. We wondered for a few hours if John killed Teresa, burned their trailer, or declared war on half the county, when John pulled up to the gas pumps out front. His face was red and there were scratch marks on his arms.

"Gimme ten dollars' worth of gas. I'm in a damn hurry. Teresa's been runnin' around with Terry, one of my buddies. Y'all look in the paper tomorrow, 'cause they's gonna be a got-dam fight in Acworth, Georgia, tonight!"

True to his word—John made the paper. He restored his honor and spent a week in jail, but did not get fired, thankfully. I guess "altercations" over your common-law wife running around with your friends were acceptable in Cassville, and Teresa never "conversated" with Terry ever again.

Dating Cassville Girls Can Be Hazardous to Your Health

Dating certain girls in Cassville could be hazardous to your health. As with most small towns, when you dated a girl, you were actually dating her whole family. You showed up at the house and everyone was there—her mama, daddy, grandparents, aunts, uncles, cousins, sisters and brothers. Even if they had known you for years, you had now entered the Bermuda Triangle of distrust. You would be vetted, quizzed, examined and evaluated by all of them. Your intentions had better be good, because if they were not, you'd find yourself in a world of hurt.

My first date was a perfect example of this. I took an interest in a girl named Christy Harmon, who lived about three miles away in a small house with her parents and younger brother. I had known this family my entire life. Her brother played baseball with my brother and spent the night at our house on several occasions. The parents came to our store on a daily basis, as did

Christy. We were on a friendly, first-name basis and always got along.

When I mustered the courage to ask her out, I paged Christy on a Friday, and she called me back about ten minutes later. Pagers were a beautiful thing in those days. Everybody who was somebody had a pager. It felt good to hear that beeping sound, it meant somebody cared about you or they were really bored. You knew you were in with a girl if they ended a page in "143."

I asked Christy to a movie, which began at 7:30 p.m. on Saturday night. She agreed excitedly and said she had to ask her parents. I heard muffled words over the phone, and I felt perspiration dripping off my forehead. Would they say no? Did they secretly not like me? What was taking so long (twelve seconds at the most)?

"Daddy said it's OK, but he wants you here early so he can talk to you."

Uh-oh. I knew what that meant. I felt nervousness all over, but I was going through with it. My truck was cleaned spotlessly, and I "Armor Alled" the hell out of the dash, seats, and steering wheel. My outfit was an ensemble of Old Navy, Timberland boots, a necklace adorned with a cross (for protection and possible body identification), and a heavy dose of Polo Sport cologne. Only the finest for Christy Harmon.

Pulling up to the house, I felt a wave of uncertainty. The only lights on were the front-porch light and the living room. The Harmons were lighting the pathway to my imminent death, I just knew it. Before I could even knock on the door, their outside dog ran up and barked maniacally at me. Mr. Harmon opened the door violently and yelled at the mutt, "Rusty, get your sorry ass back under the truck!"

"Come in," he said in a huff.

I walked into the living room, and there sat her mama, grandma, two cousins, and brother. They stared at me with heads cocked to the side, like a dog trying to figure out whether it should eat something or leave it be. No smiles, not even a nod of approval. Christy was nowhere to be found. Mr. Harmon waved me into another room, where he had various mounted animals, including a full-sized mountain lion. His flannel sleeves rolled up, showing his marine corps tattoos, he finally addressed me.

"Looka here. I know you, and I know your daddy. You're a good boy, and you ain't never given me reason to doubt you. But that's my little girl, and you know what that means. If you hurt a hair on her head, I'll be going to prison, and you'll be found in a swamp somewhere. You get me?"

"Yes, sir. I wouldn't even..." I stared at the mountain lion and Mr. Harmon's forearms, which seemed to expand every second.

"I know, but I am just letting you know. That movie got many cuss words in it?" He stared into my soul. I felt it burning like a lit cigarette being gouged into the fabric of my being.

"It's PG rated, sir." That was true. You didn't lie to men like Mr. Harmon.

"Good. I don't need Christy coming home telling us to eat shit or anything like that. Have her home by ten thirty."

He shook my hand and said, "Y'all have fun." He smiled slyly, knowing that he had killed any ill intentions that I might have had.

Christy emerged from her bedroom, looking amazing. She was very attractive and looked older than sixteen. I drove twenty miles per hour to the theater, taste-tested her stale popcorn to ensure that it was safe, said about three words to her, and had her home at 9:57. Mission accomplished, Dad.

Mr. Harmon took it easy on me, honestly. There were families who were much worse.

Ask the Coleman twins, who tried to date the sisters of Jackie Bennett and Jimmy Hill. Jackie and Jimmy were cousins who lived in the same house with about fifteen other family members. Their sisters, Ansley and Johanna, were attractive girls who guys were always chasing.

Problem was, the Hills and the Bennetts were some of the roughest people in Cassville and lived in a house that was falling apart. Windows that were not boarded up contained fans, which was a dead giveaway that meth was manufactured there. The front porch was covered with broken refrigerators, bicycles in various states of disrepair, weight-lifting equipment, and car parts. Several Native American dreamcatchers dangled from the porch ceiling—what dreams could they catch at this home of ill repute? I wasn't sure.

A rarely used tire swing swayed from a barren sweet gum tree that looked as if it would topple over any second. Their numerous mangy dogs patrolled the front yard and backyard among the inoperable vehicles, surrounded by weeds and stacks of bald tires. Random toddlers and children, covered in filth, roamed the property while the adults meandered in and out of the house in a daze. The entire scene was a Jeff Foxworthy stand-up routine.

Ansley and Johanna were the same age and were always together: walking the halls at school, at the store, cruising down in Cartersville, anywhere. The Coleman brothers were in their class at school and asked them on a double date, to which the girls agreed. Innocent enough, right?

I was working at the store when the Colemans pulled up to the house in the convertible Chrysler LeBaron they shared. The Hill/Bennett house was about fifty yards down the road, so I could see and hear anything that happened. The Colemans sat for a second as the dogs encircled their car and began their chorus of barks. Strange people in a strange car, it was a certainty that Cassville outside dogs were going to go ballistic.

This was where the Colemans began to make mistakes. Rather than getting out or trying to be friendly with the dogs, the Colemans simply honked the horn of their car to summon the girls. Wrong move. Instead, it summoned Jackie and Jimmy, who emerged in their usual uniforms of flip-flops, socks, and sweatpants, with no shirt. Despite never lifting weights or doing any sort of exercise, these two people were muscular and powerful.

"What in the *hayul* do you want?" shouted Jackie.

"Don't be honkin' your got-dam horn!" warned Jimmy.

The Colemans, renowned smart alecks, make another grievous error.

"You know why we are here. Go in the house and get Ansley and Johanna," they said in a condescending tone.

"They ain't going with y'all. Get off our driveway." Jimmy was getting annoyed.

"Oh yeah, they are. Tell 'em it's time to go." I just shook my head.

I saw Jackie and Jimmy's faces change. I had seen this change before. I saw it when Jackie was threatened by a man ten years older than him, only to have Jackie pummel him senseless in the parking lot of Big Lots. I saw it when Jimmy body-slammed another kid in the middle of a baseball game when we were children. These were not people who let things go. The more it escalated, the better for them.

Jackie and Jimmy leaped off the porch and darted toward the car, like wolves approaching wounded prey that was ready to be finished off. The topless LeBaron was suddenly a cage where the Colemans where trapped between these two angry, wild people who loved nothing more than a good fight. The yard dogs took off running in all different directions. Jackie gave the Colemans one more chance to survive this encounter.

"Get y'alls' asses out of here right now. They ain't going out with y'all."

The Colemans refused.

I shouted down to the Colemans, "Man, y'all are crazy!"

On cue, Jackie and Jimmy jumped into action. Jackie leaned in and hit one brother square on the temple, while Jimmy kicked the other in the head. Both brothers fell into each other, slumped over, and fell on the dash, knocked out cold. Jackie and Jimmy looked over at us, let out a Ric Flair "wooooooo!" and walk back into the house, as if they just walked out to check the mail.

The Colemans eventually woke up and drove off, chased by the yard dogs as they peeled out of the driveway. I never saw them on Cassville Road again.

I never went on another date with Christy, either. A week after we went to the movie, her twenty-three year old boyfriend Bubba appeared at Cass Grocery asking me about it. She somehow failed to mention she was dating one of the most frightening people I had ever known up to that point. Not only was he a giant, he had a neck tattoo and I was certain he was a drug dealer. It was no problem to agree to never speak to Christy again.

My second date went much better and she ended up being my first kiss. She was a Cassville girl too, but her family was not quite so hardcore about our dating plans. I guess they did not worry about us riding around listening to Third Eye Blind, eating Waffle House every other meal and talking on the phone all night long. There was trouble around every corner for teenagers in Cassville, but neither of us wanted our parents telling us to "go pick out a hickory switch."

CHAPTER 9

The Dramatic Life and Times
of Cigarette Smokers

THE CAMPAIGN AGAINST CIGARETTES AND smokeless tobacco washed over the country in the 1990s. Advertisements were removed from magazines and television. The surgeon general started "warning" on every pack of cigarettes and roll of snuff. Prices increased across the board, and tobacco companies started feeling the pinch of lawsuits, since it was clearly their fault that human beings had no willpower and the tobacco was forced on them.

We sold all forms of tobacco at Cass Grocery. Frankly, our store could not have survived without the sale of tobacco and alcohol. They were recession-proof items with a huge demand, and regardless of price, customers would find a way to get their hands on the next Marlboro or Budweiser. I had seen the most destitute of people dig mountains of change out of their pockets to buy a pack of Basic Light 100's—which was like smoking hot dirt. The stench alone would choke the most seasoned of garbage truck drivers.

The war on tobacco was not even waged in Cassville. Cassville was like West Virginia in the Civil War—we let everybody secede around us, and we stayed right where we were. In fact, when the big pinch on tobacco came around, our cigarette sales actually increased. It galvanized the masses against the liberals who were interfering with our rights to soak our lungs in tar and nicotine. We simply could not abide that.

Women between the ages of eighteen and thirty-five really started smoking heavily then. If Marlboro Lights needed a model smoker, then an unemployed twenty-one-year old girl from a trailer park in Cassville would be right on the money. It did not take a genius to figure it out either. They would always steal a glance at the cigarette rack as they eased through the front door—just making sure we were stocked up. With all the scientific knowledge, the health classes they took in school, and elimination of tobacco in the media, it mattered very little.

They came in waves all day long. In airbrushed "Gatlinburg 1997" T-shirts with cutoff shorts and bare feet. With an ill-fitting midriff showing off the muffin top acquired from childbirth and a tattoo of a rose just above the hip—or my personal favorite, stained pajamas that would not be removed the entire day. Lipstick that looked like it was applied while they were riding a bicycle and hair that was still matted from lying in bed, or a half-assed ponytail to disguise the fact it has not been washed in days.

She stocked up on the essentials—Fudge Rounds and Honey Buns for breakfast, as many bottles of Mountain Dew as possible, Funyuns, milk, Goody headache powders (for stress, obviously), and of course, a pack of cigarettes. If it was a particularly good week at work for her man, then she would get two packs.

Her kids would be sprinting in circles around her, fighting each other. Equipped with Kool-Aid mustaches and bare feet, they would proceed to pick up every piece of candy in the store and beg their mother to buy it. After a resounding "Hell naw, I ain't got enough for that!" she would bounce the infant with a full diaper on her hip to keep it from squealing. If the kids were bad enough, she would put the baby on the counter and give them a swat to their backsides in front of everyone.

After realizing that she did not have enough to buy everything on the counter, she put the milk back in the cooler. My dad and I would internally shake our heads at this decision, but it was not ours to make. The screaming throng exited the store— kids crying from being spanked, the baby crying from all the noise, the mother screaming at them for crying, and me carrying her groceries to her car. I negotiated the empty Mountain Dew bottles in the trunk and placed the bags inside. The family piled into the Camaro—older kids in the back, baby in the front in a car seat from 1975—and the mother furiously tore open the pack of Marlboro Lights and fired one up in ecstasy.

For men, it was much less dramatic. They came in childless with no grocery list other than cigarettes. The only time any drama came from male cigarette purchases was when we were out of his brand. Females would make do. Men simply could not fathom doing so. I saw men fall apart when I had to say, "Sorry, man, we are out until Mike comes from Cedartown tomorrow." It was like a three-act play.

Part one: "Denial."

"Gimme a pack of Winstons in a box, hoss," said Ricky, an average Cassville male.

I delivered the world-crushing news. "Sorry, Ricky. They marked 'em out on us. Can you use 'em in a soft pack?"

Dread consumed his face. Perspiration fells off his temple. His hat came off as fingers went through the hair, contemplating the issues before him. "Oh man," he exclaimed. A deep breath and a glance to the floor. "Are you serious?"

Part two: "Acceptance."

After a few seconds of thought, his eyes met mine. The people in line were getting impatient, but they got it. They were from Cassville too.

"I can't smoke them Lights, no flavor. I can't do the soft pack 'cause it'll get crushed in the truck, and they taste differ'nt anyway."

The decision-making process kicked into gear. Like a wine connoisseur picking between Chianti and Cabernet Sauvignon, he considered every pro and con. I could see his thoughts circling his head like Dale Earnhardt Jr. at Bristol. He pondered the drive to Walmart, and I must save Ricky from himself at this point.

"Ricky, I got Dorals. They are cheaper, and I have them in a box too."

No can do. "Man, them things is like smoking cardboard. There ain't no way." Cue the forlorn glance to the rack where the Winstons should be. Unlike the women, he never looked to see if I was stocked up.

Part three: "Overcoming Obstacles."

Ricky was now craning his neck to scan the rack for suitable replacements. Pawing at his chin, preparing for the most important decision he would make today. There was no margin for error. One false move and the entire day was ruined.

My eyes glazed over, but I maintained my smile.

After a deep sigh, Ricky said, "Awright, gimme a pack of Newports."

A more expensive menthol cigarette, clearly a sensible choice. I shrugged and laid them on the counter. Ricky wasted no time slamming the pack into his palm as hard as humanly possible. You must do this, or the cigarette would not smoke right, so I was told. I did not know cigarettes smoked "right" or "wrong." I apologized for being out of his brand.

"Awwww, that's OK, hoss. I smoked these things when I was in the navy. I had to switch though. These damn things'll kill ya!" He exited with a smile. The day had been saved, and Walmart lost four cents.

Underage kids were always trying to get their hands on tobacco. They would try anything and say anything to get us to sell a pack of cigarettes or can of snuff to them. There was always a story.

"Man, I'm gonna be eighteen next week."

"My mama said I could."

"I ain't gonna tell anybody."

When we would not sell to them, some resorted to creative theft. We had a bin of cheap cigarettes next to the front counter where brands like GPC, Doral, and USA Gold were piled high. The premium brands were behind us, so those were thief proof, but these cheap coffin nails were easy pickings if we turned our backs. Anytime I saw a twelve-year-old riding a bike with a Doral Light 100 dangling from his mouth, I wondered if he stole it from me.

One kid from the trailer park had a clever system, where he would ask for a dipped ice cream, and while my head was buried in the rainbow sherbet, he would swipe a couple of packs. He got away with this for a couple of weeks, but unfortunately for him, Ms. Tammy Jenkins had eagle eyes and a disdain for kids with rattail haircuts.

"That little heathern with that godawful haircut just stoled cigarettes," she whispered to me after he paid for his ice cream with a grin.

When I grabbed him by the shirt collar as he tried to pedal off on his bicycle, two packs fell from under his shirt. Score one for Ms. Tammy.

"Your mama ought to jerk a knot in your sorry tail," she huffed as she walked by.

The old guys on the benches were a hodgepodge of tobacco usage. As indicated earlier, this was a major requirement to be included in this illustrious group of Cassville's finest.

The World War II generation still puffed on nonfiltered cigarettes like Lucky Strike and Camel. Guys born in the '50s usually went for the "cowboy killers" like Marlboro Red and Winston. Some of the penny-pinching types went for Basics or other generic brands, but that was rare. You would see the line of men sitting on the bench in the morning, two trails of smoke billowing from their hands—one from their coffees and the other from their cigarettes.

Strangely enough, there was a small group of men like Daddy Kim, who smoked menthols. He supposedly quit at some point, but when he passed away, a pack of Kool Filter Kings was found behind the vice grips in his tool shed. I imagined him standing there, in his overalls, with a Kool dangling from his lips while he hammered away.

These were the same men who exhaled loudly and stared at their watches when the preacher lasted past noon on Sunday. More than an hour without a cigarette? Unacceptable.

God forbid someone walked to the altar to be "washed in the blood of the Lamb." Your soul could be saved on a random Tuesday. Let the choir get through "Turn Your Eyes upon Jesus" and the final "amen" be uttered—then witness the herd dash through the vestibules into the parking lot to light up. The Baptist church parking lot would be a cloud of smoke with a bunch of fedoras wandering around in it, complaining about how long that benediction lasted.

Those who quit smoking carried around Styrofoam cups stuffed with napkins for Skoal, Copenhagen, Red Man, and Levi Garrett. My great-grandfather dipped Bruton snuff and anytime I went to his house, I had to empty the old Hills Bros. coffee can that he spit in. It made me gag so hard, but he walked with a cane and always made time for me, so I just carried on.

Larry quit smoking years before when he woke up one morning and could not taste his food. He strategically placed his last pack of Lucky Strikes on the window sill above his kitchen sink to remind him why he quit smoking. He took up chewing Red Man immediately thereafter and went through two pouches a day. I used to beg him to let me try some, and he continually refused.

"Nancy will kill me. No way, boy." Larry loved my grandmother and did not want to make her mad.

I never let up. I thought it was cool how he would spit on the ground after explaining the intricacies of installing conduit pipe or how many gallons of diesel his backhoe could hold. Nothing punctuated a good story like a giant stream of tobacco spit.

After years of pressure, he finally caved one day and said, "All right, smartass, here you go."

I grabbed the pouch from Larry's giant hand and smelled the contents. Bliss washed over me as I smiled at Larry, who shook his head and pursed his lips. I placed the wad in my mouth, fully expecting a wave of coolness to wash over me along with instant acceptance from the bench crowd. Minutes passed by as I worked the tobacco in my mouth and spit, just like Larry. However, as time went by, the wave of coolness was replaced by something else.

I could not explain the color of green my face turned, but it was somewhere between pea soup and a bell pepper. A cold sweat covered my forehead as the faces around me started spinning. I stood up and wobbled, my stomach churning as I darted for the weeds.

"Aw, hell, he's gonna cough that shit right up," remarked Wesley through the Marlboro in his lips.

Vomit erupted from my mouth and nose. I gagged and gurgled, my eyes watering, and my heaving chest made me elicit a noise that resembled a muffler-less Camaro cranking up in the same room with a heifer giving birth.

Larry walked over, knelt down, and said, "My mama lasted longer than you did."

CHAPTER 10

Indian Outlaw and the Ice Cream Cooler

IF THERE WAS ANYTHING I could have eliminated at Cass Grocery, it would have been the hand-dipped ice cream cooler. To say I disliked this box of metal, plastic, and glass was like saying I-85 in Atlanta was pretty crowded at 5:30 p.m. in the afternoon on a weekday. I *loathed* this damn thing. When customers walked in wanting a cone, I instantly grumbled to myself and cursed their names under my breath.

In fact, there were only five things worse than dipping ice cream:

1) The song "Indian Outlaw" by Tim McGraw. I had nothing against Tim and certainly nothing against Indians (I was 1/32 Cherokee, like everyone in north Georgia), but this song was hot garbage sitting in a sauna on the planet Mercury.

2) Somebody dropping a gallon of milk on our tile floor. Many people did not know this, but a gallon of milk could cover 375 square miles. It took an hour to clean and had to be done thoroughly to prevent the unmistakable curdling smell

three days later. Undoubtedly, every single customer asked the same question, "Damn, boy, what happened?" I always wanted to say that "a cow was here and sprung a leak, but we got it stopped with some pipe glue and JB Weld."

3) The disappearance of Trapper Keepers. I had a purple one with some graffiti-looking art that was absolutely awesome.

4) Pretty much every Eddie Murphy movie not rated *R*.

5) My one and only time I tried dipping snuff. I swallowed half of it and projectile vomited on three girls in the back of a Four Runner.

How could an inanimate object cause someone such anger? It was not inanimate. It was alive, and it existed simply to drive us all crazy. Contrary to its appearance, the ice cream cooler had numerous working parts: a motor; a bay, for the scoops; with running water and a faucet; the brackets that held the product; the grips that locked the brackets to the actual box; and of course, eight three-gallon tubs of ice cream.

Then you had two kinds of sugar cones, two sizes of cups, and the napkins. It was a lot more than just a cold box. It was a menagerie of metal and plastic with the potential for 1,374,768 ways to break, leak, creak, freeze, melt, crush, pulverize, and terrorize those of us who had to deal with it. A plague upon humanity, a cacophony of dissonance—the ice cream cooler.

(It's sad that I feel this way, because I love ice cream and it gives people so much joy, but when you put up with such a disagreeable machine for sixteen years...you come to a breaking point. Everybody can relate to this if you work in an office or anywhere with machines with working parts. Even my mom hated it, and she doesn't hate anything.)

I wanted to pull a Michael Bolton and wheel the ice cream cooler out to a field and bash it with a baseball bat while Geto Boys played in the background. Instead of a PC load letter, it was broken cones at inopportune times. It was the impossibility of lining up the tubs with the brackets. It was the PVC leaking water onto the floor overnight. It was the tubs on one-half of the cooler frozen solid, and of course, five kids wanting double dips of those flavors. The issues were endless. When it was time to replace a flavor, we all groaned and sauntered to the back freezer, grabbed the newest soldier in the fight, and came back. Then the fun started.

The cooler had two brackets, which held four tubs each. These brackets were linked to the box by grips that simply locked in place by turning a knob. This knob would wedge the grip against the side of the box. No screws or nails holding it in. All it took was a hard hit, and the bracket would fall (which happened three to four times daily). I had to align all four tubs before I could lock it into place. Then I tried to lock it, but the other bracket was off kilter, so I had to take both brackets out, align all eight tubs, and try to wedge them all in together. This was nearly impossible for one person, so everybody had to turn their attention to it.

We had two men with their upper bodies stuffed into a five-by-six area, trying to turn two knobs at the same time. After twenty-three attempts, one of us had to walk away before he lost it. I swore it caused one of my coworkers to start dipping snuff again. Before we could finish this task, three people would come in and want three double-dips of chocolate. When they saw the brackets out, they would ask, "Is there something wrong with the ice cream?" My temperature would soar, and I'd see tiny imps from hell standing on top of the cooler, dancing Rockettes-style, singing "Indian Outlaw" in Fran Drescher's voice.

When I replaced a flavor, I had to remove the remaining product from the old tub. I simply took the scooper and got out as much as I possibly could. Those tubs were not cheap—as milk prices went, so went ice cream. Mayfield wasn't discount—everybody in the South knew this. You put this ice cream on top of the freshly opened tub so you could sell it first. Without fail, a person asked, "What's wrong with that ice cream on top?" or "Is that the same flavor?" Cue the imps, except one had now stopped dancing and was scraping a fork across an empty plate.

Some people did not want the "old" ice cream (less than three days), so they would request we get the ice cream from the new tub. The new ice cream had been in the back freezer, which was set at -2,876 degrees Fahrenheit, so this ice cream was harder than titanium wrapped in diamonds with a steel coating. If you dropped one of those tubs off the Empire State Building, it would go through Fifth Avenue, the igneous rock shelf below the surface, past Jimmy Hoffa's body, and straight to the earth's core. It was that hard.

I didn't hold it against people for wanting ice cream. As I said, I loved ice cream. I would stab somebody for a pistachio double-dip right now. However, customers always seemed to want ice cream the most when we were slammed and the store was busier than A-Rod's public relations guy in 2014.

I'd be outside pumping gas in a diesel truck that held forty-five gallons and checking somebody's oil and transmission, Dad would be in the hardware helping a guy with three-quarter-inch fine thread wood screws and explaining why we didn't carry metric bolts, and a church group would come in wanting ice cream. Fifteen kids ranging from five to fourteen, all wanting different sizes and flavors. More fun, especially when the youth leader looked at me and said, "*We all* want some ice cream!" I'd stare into the distance, composing myself. One imp had affixed himself on the gas pump, Riverdancing.

So after finally finishing with the gas customer and putting a quart of oil in Mrs. May's car (because she didn't trust anyone else to do it), I'd come running in, wash my hands, and saunter to the ice cream cooler. The line of children was yapping nonstop, and although they'd had five minutes to decide, they still needed to know each and every flavor.

We had the obvious flavors—no explanation was needed. This was not Baskin-Robbins or Häagen-Dazs. Cassville people usually were not hard to please in this department—chocolate, vanilla, strawberry, cherry vanilla, butter pecan, black walnut, rainbow sherbet, and cookie dough were the norm. Those flavors moved fast, and most of the time, the Mayfield rep did not bother asking what to bring. He just handed us the invoice after he was done filling the freezer. However, there was always one jackass in every group who asked, "So you guys don't have rum raisin?"

A few kids wanted to sample the chocolate, as if it had somehow changed since their last cone twenty-four hours ago. A line started to form at the register as other customers got impatient waiting for me to let fifteen kids try flavors they'd eaten 2,657 times in their young lives. I could hear the imps joyously belting out, "Half-Cherokee and Choctaw! My baby, she's a Chippewaaaawaaa. She's a one of a kind!"

So the first kids' orders: half-chocolate and half-strawberry on a cone, single vanilla in a cup, single cherry on a cone, and double sherbet in a cup. Before I finished, three things happened: (1) the single vanilla changed her mind to cherry halfway through, (2) the kid with the half-chocolate and half-strawberry dropped his cone on the floor, and (3) one of the cones, when I was dipping, shattered into six thousand pieces into the cooler.

The youth leader made a stupid joke. "Bet that happens once a day, ha!" Everybody laughed...but me. The entire line took about thirty minutes to get through. I cleaned up three spills, listened to two suggestions on flavors we should get for the future, and had to give away about 437 napkins.

Sometimes, when we were extremely busy and I didn't have time to change the tubs out, I would put a lid on an empty tub. Undoubtedly, the question came out, "What's under the lid?" So many smart-aleck remarks would pop into my head, and I would just have to beat them back. "Oh, sir, that's a new flavor called Air. You want a sample?" It finally got to the point where Dad had to write "Empty" on the lids, and still, "What *was* under there?" came out once an hour.

Then we had the elderly couples who bought ice cream every day but acted as if they'd never been there before. I would go through all eight flavors again. They would look at each other for about a minute and ponder, like somebody asked them what their social security numbers were, and finally order. If the price ever increased, which it did almost monthly, I fielded complaints. Funny though, the complaints always came from the people who needed ice cream about as much as I needed a hole in the head. It was hard to take somebody seriously who was the size of a Chevy S-10 and hyperventilated walking up one flight of stairs.

I had a fireman once order a triple-dip of butter pecan, which was the most fattening and sugary ice cream in the cooler. When I told him the price, he exclaimed, "Good Lord! That is ridiculous! I am never getting one of these again!" As I counted the chins on his face, I watched him walk out to his Tahoe, gobbling down the calorie bomb and holding his size 54 pants up. He sat down in the driver's seat, and the car lurched so hard that the ice cream fell onto his lap and rolled onto the pavement. All I could say was, "There is a God."

I look back and laugh about it now. All the times I had sticky hands, cleaning up broken cones, and picking up all the napkins that the ceiling fans blew onto the floor. Even though it caused me way more trouble than it was worth, it was all a part of working up there. Most people were easy to deal with and did not complain about the prices, and if we were really busy, they would just come back later. Still though, if you ever hear about an ice cream cooler that was left on the train tracks and completely destroyed by a high-speed locomotive…the imps did it.

CHAPTER 11

Parenting in Cassville is a Contact Sport

MILLENNIALS AND GENERATION X ARE facing attacks on all fronts these days—too much technology in our lives, too self-absorbed, too career oriented, or conversely, too dependent on our parents. We are blamed for the lack of civility in the world, the onset of ADD, and other mental diseases that did not seem to exist 20 years ago and the deterioration of education because our offspring are so rotten.

The term "boomerang" has applied to many of us, where you leave for college and then come back home after graduation to save money for your own place. Time goes by, and that temporary setup turns eerily permanent. The parents don't have the heart to give the boot, so that garage apartment becomes home.

Not my dad. I had no intention of going back, and Dad dispelled any notion quickly. As I got ready to walk across the stage with my high school class at Earl Cunningham Stadium in May 1999, he laid it on the line.

"Well, congratulations, son. You got two choices now—Athens, Georgia, or Parris Island, South Carolina. Take your pick."

Mom always hated that. My age never mattered to her. I think if she had her way, I would have stayed in my old room until I was thirty-seven.

That was not exactly what Dad meant. It was just a message that I was not hanging around Cassville in my early twenties. I was already accepted at the University of Georgia and had my dorm assignment on the second floor of Creswell Hall. I was physically in Cassville for the next three months, but my mind was already at football games, meeting new friends, and my new life as an "adult."

That summer was not so bad though. I worked at the store during the day, and at night I would page various friends and get into mischief. When we figured out how to send messages with the numbers, it was like an epiphany. I became an expert very quickly. My all-time greatest was figuring out "I have stretch-marks," a message sent by an unlucky female to one of my basketball teammates. He looked at me and said, "Awwww, hell naw." My skills ended that relationship.

After cruising around Town Center Mall or going to this God-awful dance club called Cantina, we would make the thirty-minute drive back home for the real fun. No road sign was safe from us, and my friend Danny's Toyota truck bed would clang all night long from our adventures. In Cassville, there was a Confederate Street sign that we victimized monthly. The county, for some unknown reason, put a sign on both ends of this barely paved road that was no more than seventy-five yards long.

The only signs of life on this tiny road was an abandoned barn full of old tilling equipment, and Mr. Atwood's house. He was a renowned bootlegger who kept a stash of beer and liquor for Sunday drinkers on his porch. After church on Sunday, you could set your watch to the number of pickup trucks that would ease down Confederate Street and park in his driveway. He got busted every six months, and his name and address would be posted in the local paper, which was like a free advertisement.

If my eye doctor held up the vision test on one end and I stood on the other, I would pass it. We would get both of the signs and give the fruits of our labor to friends, who would hang them up in their rooms or over barn doors.

This carried on until late July, when I totally lost my nerve after an ill-fated snatch-and-grab mission orchestrated by yours truly. There was a Peachtree Road on the south side of Cartersville. I decided to take it and claim that we had driven to Atlanta and taken it from a busy intersection. If anything was clear about Atlanta, there were about 4,675 roads called "Peachtree." I really never understood it, and it confused the hell out of natives and tourists alike.

"Take Peachtree Road until you come to Peachtree Lane. Take a right, and then make a left on Peachtree Corners Circle, and you will see Peachtree Plaza on the left next to Peachtree Movers."

We waited until "pitch dark" to spring into action. The Toyota creeped up and sat under the tall sign, one that I could not reach by jumping off the bed of the truck. I was going to leap and grab the sign and use my body weight to pull it down. I stepped on the tire and positioned myself to take this Holy Grail of road signs. I could already hear my friends marveling over my false bravery. The door was open, and Danny excitedly said, "Get that sumbitch!" I crouched and got ready to leap off the truck. For some reason, I looked straight ahead, and my guts sank to my feet. A police car, complete with one deputy, sitting in plain sight. As luck would have it, he was looking down at a notepad on the steering wheel. I could not stop in midleap, so I fell off the truck and rolled into a ditch filled with stagnant water.

Danny freaked out. "Man, what the hell?"

I scrambled out of the ditch and crawled into the cab of the truck, panting and yelling "go!" As he made a right, I pointed to the cop car. Danny let out a string of expletives that would make a drill instructor blush. He had to pull over at the Golden Gallon gas station about a mile down the road and gather himself. I was covered in foul water and totally panicked. We made eye contact and saw our impending college careers flash before our eyes.

"No more." We said that unison. The signs we had were taken to the deepest depths of the woods of Cassville and disposed. He moved to Atlanta three weeks later, and I left for Athens soon thereafter, both cities spared from the "Yote" (the nickname of his truck) and two idiots who could not handle boredom.

I was fairly certain our parents knew we were into mischief. Matt and his closest friends nicknamed themselves "Two Run Creek Mafia." The sole purpose of this organization was to cause havoc and mayhem. They covered a "See Ruby Falls" sign with a giant tarp adorned with the spray-painted words "Big Daddy," where it remained for weeks.

There was nothing else to do, other than hang around the Waffle House all night. In a small town, we had to make our own fun sometimes, and that meant taking risks and getting into trouble. As my great-uncle Lindsey told my dad when I was born, "Aww, you got a boy. That's good. Boys are born with a lot of shit in 'em. You just gotta beat it out of 'em." Thanks a lot, Uncle Lindsey.

Corporal punishment and merciless berating were acceptable protocols in Cassville. The adage "be seen and not heard" applied to children between the ages of two and fifteen. Once you got to the sixteen to eighteen range, the adage "just don't embarrass us" took over. However, no matter how old you got, your mama was always right, and Daddy could still whup your ass.

The store was the sight of many arguments among families because being in public meant nothing to these folks. I saw unruly boys get dragged from the candy rack and get spanked over by the cheap canned dog food. You could almost see the basset hound pictured on the cans grimace at the sight of Wanda beating little Cody's rear end like she was possessed by Lucifer himself.

These mothers would bring small children into our store and expect them not to want candy and ice cream. Dad and I strategically placed the candy in a child's line of sight, so this was a futile expectation. Once kids inevitably asked for a Snickers bar, Skittles, or Twix, the tirade would start.

"I done told you—get over here!"

The exasperation in the mother's voice was overwhelming, as if the child asked the mother to recite the Constitution in Swahili.

Cassville women were often in a hurry, for unexplained reasons. When you were wearing a muumuu and bedroom slippers at 3:37 p.m., chances were you had not accomplished anything of use that day. Chances were good that you did not leave the couch as Maury, Jerry, and Judge Judy contaminated your brain in between ads for personal injury attorneys and the newest commemorative Elvis plate for three easy installments of $19.99.

However, these were the folks in the biggest hurry and always annoyed with their small children, who inconveniently decided to return home after school. As soon as her kids walked in our door, their mama was already shouting threats.

"Don't y'all *even* think about gettin' no candy!"

"What about ice cream, Mama?"

"Hell naw!"

Then the child would start touching the candy, a huge no-no.

"Git your damn hands off that!"

All of this took place as she stocked up on Fudge Rounds, Mountain Dew, and Marlboro Lights for herself. After all, long days of watching DNA test results, chairs flying at cheating boyfriends, and plaintiffs winning $327 in lawsuits over siphoning gas out of go-carts in Arkansas would take it out of you.

One lady in particular, Candy, was in a perpetual state of anger with her three children: Tommy, Crissy, and an infant girl that I never heard her call anything but "Little Bit." Candy was slender in build, but I was pretty sure she was made out of tire irons and axle grease. Her outfits consisted of cutoff shorts or jeans with a black T-shirt that either had a race car driver or a quote like "I'm Not a Morning Person."

I never knew her age. She was one of those people who could be forty or twenty-five. Her skin was ghostly white, she was missing several teeth, and her hair was always matted down like she washed it with Crisco. She probably got her first tattoo in elementary school and was either conceived in a rent-by-the-hour hotel room or a conjugal visit in prison. I had never seen a female who could smoke more cigarettes or take as many Goody headache powders in a day.

Her husband, Danny, was an auto mechanic/part-time drug dealer who appeared to be more afraid of Candy than getting caught dealing crank in every trailer park east of Cherokee County. He had a ponytail, a beard, a wallet with a chain, and wore his work shirt with his name on it all day. When he got home, he'd unbutton it, and his gut poked out when he walked around. He was actually semi-intelligent but hid it behind a layer of barley, hops, and using a little of his own product. I could tell because his eyes would be wider than a soup bowl, and he would say "hey, man, hey" about a thousand times before he'd get to the point of the conversation.

This family was a train wreck of epic proportions. Crammed into a trailer just off Highway 41 and surrounded by relatives identical to them in many ways. The kids were a combination of both parents. Tommy had a smart mouth and wore the same shirt every other day, covered in filth. Crissy had a perpetual Kool-Aid mustache, pale skin, and answered yes or no questions with a snarl that would make R. Lee Ermey proud. I thought the infant told me to "eat shit" once.

Sundays were always fun because Danny would be watching NASCAR, drunk as a skunk. Undoubtedly, he would ask Candy to go to the store for supplies halfway through the race. Rather than leave the little hellions at home, she'd pile them up and take them to the store. She would agree to let them actually get candy this time. Of course, they'd take forever (more than twelve seconds) to decide, especially Crissy. This was an issue that exasperated Candy, who wanted to get back and watch the last 6,787 laps of the race.

"Crisssssyyyyyy! Gitchey sumpin! The race is on! Your daddy is waitin'!"

Candy would scream at the kids and utter profanity that would make the men on the benches grimace. Those kids could do nothing right, and I often wondered why she let them come in. Strangely, after she'd tell Tommy to "get your damn hands off them Twix bars," she'd look at me and say, "Sweetie, lemme get two packs of Danny's cigarettes and two packs of mine."

(Often, cigarettes at Cass Grocery lost their proper name after a while, and they would become the property of a customer. "Ricky's cigarettes" were Kool Filter Kings. "James's cigarettes" were Basic Menthol. Or you could get really removed and have "Ed's daddy's cigarettes," which were Basic Ultra Light 100's... because he was trying to quit, of course.)

The older kids would be running in circles around the candy rack as she would fruitlessly threaten them. Then she would finally catch one by the arm, sit Little Bit on the counter, and spank them so hard on the ass that they would swing up in the air. I had seen those kids beaten mercilessly, and they would come back for more every day. Little masochists.

Tommy brought a Super Soaker in once and squirted Crissy, who squealed to high heaven. Candy took the gun and hit him across the back with it and then threw it into the parking lot. All of this took place in front of at least fifteen people. He ran out crying into the street. Candy grabbed Little Bit and snatched Crissy up by the arm, even though she was innocent, and slung them all into the truck. You could see her driving with one hand and beating Tommy as she peeled out of the parking lot. You could see the airbrushed bumper sticker that aptly read "Redneck Bitch" as she disappeared down Cassville Road.

In Candy's defense, she was brought up hard. Her father was nicknamed "Mountain Man" and spent ten years in prison for slicing a man's throat after cheating in a card game. He had the words "sweet" and "sour" tattooed over his nipples and actually had a list of women inscribed on his left arm, with his former "old ladies" marked out with an *X*. Candy's mom was about the third one marked out, but they got back together, so he had her name replaced on the list.

Eventually, Candy and Danny split up because Candy was sleeping with his brother Rodney, who lived next door. They ended up getting married, and Danny floundered around Bartow County until he ended up in jail. Rodney had three rotten little kids too, so Candy was screaming and hollering double time now. That rocked on for a few years, but I guess that became too much, and Candy bailed out totally. She dyed her hair jet black, became a lesbian, and lived with her girlfriend on the other side of town. She did not scream anymore, seemed happier than ever...but she still had the "Redneck Bitch" bumper sticker.

CHAPTER 12

Dale Earnhardt Never Drank Mike's Hard Lemonade

"HEY, MAN, WHO'S WINNIN' THE race?"

If I heard that question once on Sundays, I heard it a million times. Cassville men loved NASCAR. They lived for the sound of engines, tires squealing, and announcers saying things like "Earnhardt comes outta turn four like a slingshot to take the lead from Swervin' Ernie Irvan."

Our thirteen-inch television that faced the cash register and the candy rack so customers could see what we were watching. The content depended on who was working that day.

If Dad was there, it was always some form of news. He owned the place, and that was that—a day of foreign policy, local weather, traffic, taxes, crime, and opinions on how bad the president and Congress sucked last week. The guys on the benches would often prop up on the stacks of twelve-pack Cokes and watch the news with him. Of all the topics discussed, nothing started more debates than the weather.

"They said it rained three-quarters of an inch last night, but my rain gauge had a full inch. Man, they don't know nothin' down there in Atlanter."

Because every man had a rain gauge and every one of them contained a different amount of precipitation, they would argue over who was more correct. Apparently, the future of the earth and life as we knew it was predicated on the accuracy of this information. I saw friendships become strained over arguments about humidity and dew points.

If Dad was not working, the television became a Pandora's box of programming. If it was a weekday afternoon, I would always catch *Saved by The Bell* and then find sports or a decent movie. Saturday mornings were devoted to Dean Durham, Bill Dance, Jimmy Houston, or Shaw Grigsby ensnaring various wildlife across the country. This would always draw a crowd and farfetched stories of past hunting and fishing expeditions.

"Awww, man, that ain't nothin' compared to the bass I got over at Lake Weiss!" Then the story would continue, dripping with enthusiasm and bald-faced lies.

Eventually, this bass would be three-feet long, 345 pounds, and run the forty-yard dash in 4.3 seconds. Welcome to Cassville—our deer were faster, our fish were bigger, the beards on our turkeys were longer, and our Carolina rigs were tied better.

One guy, Robert, took a shark-fishing trip to Brunswick, Georgia, with his friends. They got drunk all day on the boat. He caught a nine-foot long tiger shark and decided it was a good idea to bring it into the boat. (Sharks are made of concrete and teeth, by the way.) It thrashed around until his sixteen-foot boat was completely destroyed and sank into the Atlantic Ocean. The coast guard had to rescue four drunks floating in the water with an angry man-eater. Brilliant.

Without fail, any fish story would always gravitate to the legendary giant catfish at the dam on Allatoona Lake. I was sure every southern lake had a similar tale—our very own Loch Ness monster. Apparently, this unseen catfish was so big that it ate a johnboat with a trolling motor. Some guy, whose name nobody could remember, tried to catch it with the winch on his Jeep and a bloody chicken carcass attached to a meat hook. The catfish dragged the Jeep into the lake, and it was never found.

But on Sundays, the television must be tuned to the NASCAR race. This was not negotiable. One of our new employees turned the channel to the Falcons game during a race at Bristol, and I thought guns would be drawn. These men could not care less about the Dirty Birds or the Georgia Dome. It was the Intimidator, Handsome Harry Gant, Rusty, Darrell, Mark, Dale Jarrett, and their hatred of Jeff Gordon that enamored them.

Jeff Gordon was considered too "purty" for NASCAR, and it did not help that he was from California or that his car was a multicolored rainbow sponsored by a company with a French name. When he burst on the scene, it was like drinking flat Coke and eating cold grits. To say they disliked Jeff Gordon was like saying the Grand Canyon was a big ditch. They *loathed* this man—he did not cut his teeth on dirt tracks in Georgia, chew tobacco, drink, cuss, and fight his way to the top. He was a rich boy who went out and bought himself a race team.

As much as they despised Gordon, they loved Dale Earnhardt Sr. with the same intensity. He was a linthead from North Carolina, and many Cassville people could relate to his humble beginnings. Whatever he did was legendary. Whatever he said was law. And if anyone disagreed with him, they "ain't from around here" and probably drank Mike's Hard Lemonade with their pinkies up.

In fact, I was convinced that Dale could have endorsed the following five things and Cassville men would have fallen in line faster than the church crowd driving to Ryan's Mega Bar on Sunday afternoon:

1) Calvin Klein pink thong underwear for men
2) Fat free Yogurt or hummus
3) Yoga classes
4) Hypercolor T-Shirts
5) Celine Dion's latest album

Pee Wee Reynolds lived in a trailer park near me, and he worshiped at the church of Earnhardt weekly. I never saw Pee Wee without his "3" hat on and a T-shirt listing all of his racing accomplishments. Hell, Pee Wee probably got married on pit road at Dixie Speedway in Woodstock, Georgia.

His wife cranked their station wagon one night, and it back-fired. Flames from the exhaust pipe somehow hit a can of kerosene, which exploded and engulfed the side of their trailer in flames. Realizing the home would be a total loss, Pee Wee salvaged what he could that night by dashing into the trailer and tossing items into the back of his truck.

The following day, he pulled up to the store in his pickup with his wife and four kids in the cab. The Reynolds were on the move to greener pastures after their home was reduced to ashes. In the back of the truck was a bunch of Earnhardt T-shirts, a portrait of Earnhardt at Daytona, a signed racing helmet, and his wife's ironing board. Everything else was consumed by the inferno.

Grown men would dash out of their trucks in their Sunday best to catch a glimpse of our TV and confirm if their driver was in the hunt. Commentary was imminent.

"Aw hell, that damn Jeff Gordon is leading."

"Bill's gotta make a run, he ain't won Talladega in awhile."

"I seen Ernie Irvan in the Waffle House outside of Chattanooga, he's a good ol' boy."

"Dadgummit. Dick Trickle wrecked, I didn't even see him drive. I knew Gladys played "Because He Lives" too long."

The popularity of stock car racing has waned in recent years and I know the reason. NASCAR has abandoned its roots. Cassville men cannot relate to Jimmy Johnson or Kyle Busch. NASCAR has taken races out of the South and added them in places like Las Vegas and California. For the good men of Cassville, those races might as well be in Asia. It is sad to see a brand going global and forgetting that it all started in 1979 when two small town Southern boys duked it out on the infield at the Daytona 500.

At least Pee Wee Reynolds still has his ironing board.

CHAPTER 13

Peach's for Sale and Pawpaw's Serjury

IN LARGE CITIES ACROSS AMERICA, it seems that construction is being done on every block, every single day. New York City is covered in scaffolding and plywood walls that block the job site from the public eye and reroute pedestrian traffic. Spray-painted on these walls in large stenciled letters are the three words "Post No Bills."

Those words mean no signage is to be affixed to these temporary force fields. No advertisements. No concert posters. No offers for guitar lessons, house cleaning, or learning Spanish. If signs are posted overnight, which they often are, the workers tear them down as soon as they report for duty the next morning. You could see the corners of the paper hanging in the T50 staple that remained in the wood afterward. I often wondered what message the deceased sign was conveying.

It astounds me that New York abides in this practice. The place most concerned with the free flow of ideas and the most thriving bastion of capitalism in the world allows this communism to take place. Half of the city is covered in these plywood walls, and they are barren wastelands of thought and commerce. When you see scaffolding going up, you might as well be in Red China standing in front of a tank in Tiananmen Square.

No such communism existed at Cass Grocery. The flow of ideas washed over 1810 Cassville Road like the Mississippi River after a week of rain. Far be it from us to stop our fellow citizens from getting the word out about important events taking place or offering their services to the public. Any time somebody walked through our door with a roll of masking tape and a sign and asking if they could post it, the answer was always "Yes, the Coke machine is wide open."

Coca-Cola placed a vending machine on the front of the store, between one of the benches and the propane tank storage area. It wasn't there until the early 90's because Dad was afraid it would be robbed every night. Cassville was so quiet in those days that somebody could take thirty minutes to break into that machine in the middle of the night and nobody would see them. However, other than graffiti and scratching, the vending machine held firm all those years.

You could see where people tried to break into it to no avail, the telltale bending of metal where a wayward crowbar lost its battle at three o'clock in the morning. You could imagine the meth-head walking back down Cassville Road in the dark, defeated and dejected that he could not steal the $5.40 sitting in the change box just out of his reach. Those machines were like diamonds wrapped in titanium—they weren't getting through that.

Although our Coke rep hated the fact that we allowed signage to cover the vending machine, there was nothing he could do about it. He would periodically ask Dad about it, and Dad would dismiss him immediately. There was no way that he was going to stop people or tear their signs off the Coke machine. In fact, my dad was the de facto keeper of the American way up there. He let all politicians place signs on our property, even those he had no intention of voting for.

That Coke machine became the community bulletin board of Cassville. It was also a perfect example of how we southerners could lay waste to the English language with the skill of a surgeon. My seventh grade language-arts teacher would have had a conniption fit (an old-school southern term, not to be confused with a hissy fit) reading some of these literary abominations.

(A conniption fit is one of anger—if the drive shaft of your 1987 Dodge Ram falls apart on Highway 41, if Jeff Gordon wins the Daytona 500, or if your kids get arrested vandalizing a Waffle House, you are entitled to a conniption fit. A hissy fit is one of whining—when your kids are told they cannot go to the county fair because they stole your cigarettes and smoked them at a church lock-in, when QVC overcharges Wanda for the commemorative Aunt Bea plate, or when gas prices increase by one cent, the offended party is entitled to one hissy fit.)

"Peach's for Sale" (apparently these are emancipated "peach's," since they own themselves).

"House for Sell, Buy Owner" (you can have the owner with the house, if you ever "sale" it).

"Larry's Lawn Care and Maintenants" (any tenants not of the main variety are unacceptable).

"Benifit for Papaw's Serjury" (you could substitute Mawmaw, Pee Wee, Monkey, Leon, or Weevil here)

"Gerage Sell—Make Your Best Ofer" (I got nothing here. God bless us).

Many of these were handwritten on poster board in black marker. You could tell when a man wrote them because they were barely legible with random capitalization and punctuation spread throughout.

"Yard Sell AT Pine LoG Road, take LeFt on Grogan, Road and right at The broke down ford. First trailer on the right. watch out for Chows and Rockwallers." (Chows and Rottweilers permeated Cassville like mosquitoes in a stale puddle of water in a used tractor tire. You could drive down any road on the former Rural Route 3 without being chased by one or the other.)

Also, the first words of the message were much larger because the man did not realize how quickly the space ran out on the poster board. Hence, the words at the bottom typically required a magnifying glass to read them.

Other popular residents on the Coke machine were promotions for upcoming wrestling events. This was not WWE, however. There were no Vince McMahons or Hulk Hogans. This was North Georgia Outlaw Wrestling touting a chainsaw match between Ricky "Sugar Daddy" Sanford and Randy "The Masked Assassin" Haney—two guys who probably bought their costumes at Walmart in Ellijay two hours before the match being held at the old Fairmount Elementary School gym.

Whomever was victorious in the chainsaw match would be able to hoist the coveted Georgia-Alabama-Tennessee Outlaw

Heavyweight Championship Belt. I could think of nothing better than returning to hero's welcome in Armuchee, Georgia, with that belt in the passenger seat of my Firebird. In two weeks, you got to defend your crown in the Dairy Queen parking lot in Jasper, against Leroy "The Calhoun Cutthroat" Davis.

(Crowd involvement was always an issue at these things. If the heel got thrown into the crowd, a smuggled bottle of Miller High Life could find itself smashed on his forehead. You must remember, these people truly believe that wrestling was real. They also believe that cigarettes in a box smoke differently than those in a soft pack, still call super unleaded gasoline "high test," and think that Pink Floyd is a gay bar in Atlanta.)

Dad did not allow posters inside the store. He did, however, allow people to seek donations by way of Mason jar on our counter. This is common in most country stores in the South. You have seen the jars with the pictures and the sad story of someone with a rare disease or their home was destroyed by Mother Nature. One of those donation jars caused a fistfight in Cassville.

The child of a seventeen-year old girl was seriously injured when, during a family party, the child crawled behind the car of a drunk leaving the party. I had seen this child plenty of times—diaper always full, Kool-Aid mustache 24/7, and probably Mountain Dew or Yoo-hoo in its bottle. Blame flew everywhere. The rumor began to fly around that the family actually did it on purpose to collect the insurance money. Tensions got high around the trailer park. The mother, perpetually barefoot and pregnant with another baby, came to the store moping around and placed a donation jar on our counter. All I could think was, "Oh great, you procreated again."

Well, baby daddy was not in the picture, unbeknownst to us. These girls went through boyfriends like emancipated peaches being sold in Adairsville. These guys all looked exactly alike and had the same names—skinny, white, wearing a T-shirt two sizes too big, a chain necklace adorned with a skull or an AK-47, a backward "No Fear" hat, and a neck tattoo. Nothing says "I don't give a damn about a career" like a neck tattoo. Every one of them was named Johnny, Jason, Shane, Shawn, or the quadruplet of initials (AJ, BJ, CJ, or DJ). They wandered from town to town, crashing with random barefoot, pregnant girls to get their hands on the government checks.

In this case, baby daddy got wind of the injury to his beloved child and ended his sabbatical from fatherhood quicker than a Baptist preacher's benediction at 11:59 a.m. (In the old days, the men would glance at their watches and sigh loudly. This was the universal signal to wrap it up. My great-grandfather, my grand-father, my great-uncles, and all their friends would dash out the door and light up their Lucky Strikes and Chesterfields as fast as humanly possible.)

Baby daddy materialized in Cassville in his burned-out Mustang to assert his sadness and disappointment that baby mamma could be so careless. Maybe the child would be better off living in whatever hourly hotel or meth house that baby daddy was shacking up in. After all, if you could not trust perpetually barefoot, uneducated seventeen-year old girls named Chastity or

Charity (who were neither charitable nor chaste), who could you trust?

After a huge falling-out, certainly over the welfare of the child, baby daddy made his rounds and stole every donation jar from every store in the county, including the one we had. He returned to the trailer park, and baby mamma's current boyfriend saw the jars on the floorboard, and attacked. He smashed the driver's-side window and tried to get baby daddy in his grasp. Baby daddy slammed the accelerator to the floor and held his attacker's arm and drove several yards with him until he fell off.

The only reason I knew this was because the boyfriend came to the store and bought some beer to ease the pain of his arm, mangled by the broken window. (I will give credit where it is due—the socks tied around his wound were clean.) He said he was going to go to the emergency room, but North Georgia Outlaw Wrestling was coming to Kingston that night, and he did not want to miss the ladder match.

CHAPTER 14

"Git on It" is Cassville's "E Pluribus Unum"

"GIT ON IT!"

If I heard that command shouted to the heavens in Cassville once, I heard it a million times. This three-word sentence was a weapon of empowerment. A recipe for excitement and possible destruction. An invitation to cut loose, forget the world, the rules, your wallet, and possibly get arrested or become a legend in the annals of Cassville history.

When people decided to "git on it," they were showing the world how far up the ladder of success they had climbed. How little regard they had for their own safety, the ever-watchful eyes of sheriffs' deputies, or the costs of the choices they were about to make. Urged on by compatriots from the benches of Cass Grocery, caution and billowing smoke were thrown into the wind to the sound of "hoopin' and hollerin'" from those encouraging this behavior.

Yes, they were laying drag.

(For those ignorant souls or those who misunderstand, laying drag takes on many names—"par [power] lockin'," "burnin' rubber," or "gettin' a wheel" will suffice as a moniker for this pastime. It may seem inconsequential or foolish to those who inhabit urban areas or value their tires' condition over the adoration of throngs of small-town southerners, but in Cassville, "gittin' on it" has taken on a life of its own.)

The make, model, or condition of the vehicle mattered not, although muscle cars and older model pickup trucks were typically preferred. In Cassville, we were equal opportunity drag layers, and anyone who chose to abide by the spirited requests of the Cass Grocery bench mob was welcomed. Whether it be a late '80s Camaro, a 1997 Mazda Protégé, a 1989 Chevy Silverado with no mufflers, a tricked-out Honda Civic, or a Volkswagen Beetle—we were excited when things went our way.

The protocol was simple, really.

The intersection had four pathways to glory for drag layers, but the most successful had always come from the east and west sides, where the road was slightly inclined. This incline gave the vehicle more ability to gain traction and smoke the tires quite nicely. Still, I had witnessed some good ones from all sides that turned our quiet corner into a rubber-scented den of iniquity that had some people complaining, but most of the time we heard "Man, that was a good 'un" from even the most passive of Cassville folks.

Once you pulled up to one of the four stop signs, your eyes would inevitably find the store and the benches out front. If there was a group of young and old men sitting around, there was a chance you'd see one another. Once eye contact was made, this was the moment of truth. Would you be summoned to entertain the masses or allowed to pass undetected by the rubber-craving male population?

If you were chosen, one or more would stand and take at least two steps toward your vehicle. As he came to a stop in your view, his two index fingers would point at each other, and a circular motion would ensue. Some were more enthusiastic and rotated their forearms over one another. Regardless of the physical motion, there was one thing they had in common—the command "git on it!"

Now, you had a choice. You could shake your head and continue to your destination, or you could possibly wreck the car, get a flat tire, or get pulled over by a sneaky deputy approaching out of your line of sight. A four-second moment of weakness could cost you some serious money and time if you were not careful.

However, you knew you would be branded as less than a man. You probably listened to Celine Dion, watched *The Bachelor*, and drank Mike's Hard Lemonade through a straw while wearing yoga pants. Comments would fly around like lightning bugs in an empty pasture on a hot July night.

"I knew he wouldn't. His wife done got him on *lockdown*, boy."

"He done turned sissy. Look at him. Been goin' to 'Lanter too much."

"Psssh. He ain't got time for us now. Gotta get home and count his money."

That cost way more than money. The scorn of your fellow Cassvillians knew no bounds. The next time you came in, they were likely to call you "sweetheart" or, worse, "city boy." My advice was to oblige them and cook your tires without hesitation. You could find yourself unwelcome and banished to the suburbs, driving a Plymouth Voyager.

Then there were others who needed no such prodding. In fact, many would pull up to the intersection with every intention of smoking the tires down to the rim. You knew it would be a good one when you heard the engine rev and shift to neutral. You got the slow nod from the driver—with a look that said "Hey, y'all, watch this." These were true Cassville people.

Once this took place, there was no stopping it. This was the Cassville man in his true, natural habitat. The back tires started spinning and smoke began pouring from under the chassis. Those perched on the bench jumped around like their heads were on fire and their asses were catching (+1 for the Charlie Daniels reference). Rebel yells and high fives abounded as the vehicle began fishtailing forward down Cassville Road and as the driver leaned out the window with a Ric Flair "wooooooo!"

Matt and I were not heavy hitters in the "git on it" game. We drove Ford Rangers that "couldn't pull a greased string out of a cat's ass," as Rusty said. My engine was so weak, I had to turn the air conditioning off if a road had a steep incline. Neen would roll her eyes at our foolishness and tell us "y'all quit that and come help me get these euonymus bushes watered."

My friend Pete was famous for his skills and he destroyed more tires than all the other daredevils combined. He was one of those who needed no encouragement, just a look of approval.

Pete *loved* to "git on it;" hell, he lived for it. It did not hurt that he drove a Chevrolet 1500 truck with a light bed and an enormous engine—the perfect recipe for burning rubber with a vengeance. Our screams and high fives fueled Pete's desire to prove himself. As he would leave the store, he would always say, "Hey, y'all, I'm 'bout to git on it for real out here."

He had the worst luck though. He almost destroyed his dad's truck, smoking the tires in our school's back parking lot. This parking lot was the size of Rhode Island and was completely empty except for one tiny brick structure housing some electrical equipment. For some reason, Pete got on it within twenty feet of this building, and the tires caught traction, sending the truck into the building. You could have had a football game complete with bleachers and a marching band between that building and the next closest structure.

My favorite Pete incident came one afternoon in the summer of 2001. It was a quiet, boring day, and Pete was on his way home from work. He stopped in to get some food, and as he was leaving, I said, "Hey, Pete, burn them tires up on your way out."

My words only served to ignite him, and he said, "I'm gonna set off y'alls' smoke alarm."

Pete backed out and pointed the truck northward and began to spin the tires furiously. We ran out the door and danced around the smoking truck—I was barking and howling like a rabid dog while my coworker was screaming "git on it" as loud as humanly possible. As Pete slowly came out of the fishtail, a police officer in full SWAT gear walked from a house into the road and held up his hand. In his most country voice, he bellowed, "Boah, pull your ice over in the parking lot *rot now*!"

The cops were busting a family meth operation two houses down, and we made enough noise to draw them away from the tweakers and dangerous chemicals to initiate a traffic stop on Pete. He sat there for two hours while the cops finished loading up the evidence and throwing the criminals in the paddy wagon. One of the eldest sons tried to run, and he was slammed onto one of the four inoperable Mustangs in the front yard. The mother, in a nightgown and hair curlers, was screaming and threatening the SWAT members with a rolling pin.

The officer wrote Pete a ticket with his Colt AR-15 rifle on his shoulder, chewing him out the whole time.

It did nothing to faze Pete. After the officers were out of sight, Pete backed out and absolutely unleashed the greatest drag laying in the history of Cass Grocery. His truck was completely lost in smoke. Our windows were open, and the wind blew the smoke into the store, and our alarm went off, just as Pete had promised. He shot us a bird as we saw the back windshield disappear down the road.

One of the meth family members who survived the police raid came out and said, "Dang, that boy can git on it, can't he?"

CHAPTER 15

Swarming Wawstes and Big John's Exhaust—the Perils of Pumping Gas

"Y'ALL GOT ONE ON THE front!"

That was what Dad would yell when a vehicle thirsty for gasoline pulled next to our pumps. As one of the last full-service stations around, we had a reputation to uphold, so we dropped whatever we were doing and sprinted outside. We could not keep the ladies and gentlemen of Cassville waiting.

Pumping gas and checking oil at Cass Grocery was a universe unto itself. A world of possibilities and a window into the lives of the citizens of Cassville. A person's vehicle was often a reflection of his or her character and background.

You could hear them flying down Cassville Road, as loud as a Def Leppard concert, coming our way. To make the car sound louder without breaking the bank, the muffler was removed. They'd pull up and look at me, rev the engine, and remark, "Sounds good, don't it?" I just had to smile and nod—these folks were our lifeblood.

"Gimme five dollars' worth, young'in, and check my oil if you can." (Imagine getting five dollars in gas today. You might be able to back out of your driveway and make it to the nearest Waffle House.)

Back then, five dollars went much further, and it was a common request at the store. Most people never filled their cars up. They got just enough to get to their next destination and back home again. I could not understand the economics behind this, but it worked out pretty well for us because they always remembered something else they needed to buy.

Removing the gas cap was an adventure sometimes. For many Cassville people, gas caps disappeared, and less conventional methods were used to cover their tanks. I had removed rags, wadded up newspaper, balls of duct tape, a bundle of very small sticks taped together and shoved into the hole, cellophane, aluminum foil, socks, and once, a pair of granny panties.

"Hell, man, them dang kids took my cap" was often the excuse. I wasn't sure what a kid wanted with a gas cap, but the drawers and closets of the children of Cassville obviously were rife with wayward gas caps. Kids were also blamed for the trash bag doubling as the passenger window and the coat hanger holding down the hood. Creativity was the name of the game when masking deformities on their IROC Camaro with 256,000 miles on it.

Sometimes, I was handed a screwdriver to pry the gas door open. When I was in middle school, I popped the door open on a Firebird that had been sitting in a man's yard for about three years. As soon as the door flew open, about eight wasps (or "wawstes," in Cassville vernacular) chased me away, and all the passengers in the car bailed out. The entire tank opening was covered by a nest of them. (You have not lived until you have sprayed Raid on a car just so you can pump two dollars of gas into it.)

We had those old pumps with glass panels covering the spinning numbers and with motors housed underneath. When we reset the pump, the numbers all spun back to 0.00. Occasionally we would have to lubricate the parts so the numbers would spin accurately. There was no credit card swiping, computers asking for zip codes, or "Receipt: Y/N?" I thought people liked the old-school approach and seeing the old pumps in action. It was something big truck stops and Walmart could not provide.

Mr. Massey always asked for ten dollars of Unleaded Plus because he claimed "that high test would burn my engine up." Mr. Fowler would fill up his vomit-colored Dodge Dart and tip me a quarter to get his Camel cigarettes, which he lit up while his oxygen tank rode shotgun next to him. Mrs. Cantrell was so flighty that she never parked on the correct side of the pump and always wanted her transmission checked, which I would do three or more times a week.

We all learned the utility of cat litter out there. When an old-timer had a truck that could not handle the speed of the pump, it would cough gasoline all over the concrete and our hands. Dad stored an open bag of cat litter in the back room, and we quickly covered the puddle before some fool threw a lit Marlboro on it and blew us to kingdom come. Every single time, the customer would say, "You ain't gonna charge me for that spilt gas, are ye?" (No, sir, we will deduct four cents off your bill.)

One guy, Big John, drove a Dodge truck that might have been manufactured during Teddy Roosevelt's presidency. Big John looked like an evil character from the *Lord of the Rings*, with his inexplicable dark tan, curly black hair, consistently shredded T-shirts, and boots that looked as if he'd tossed them in a wood chipper before putting them on. He smelled like a cross between a gym bag and catfish guts that had sat in an empty cooler for a week. If a woman saw him coming toward her, she would probably pepper spray him. Problem was, John was the nicest guy in the world.

The truck was about twelve shades of brown with primer gray and black mixed in on the quarter panels. It was made of pure steel and rust. (He once totaled a Dodge Stealth backing out of a parking spot at the Waffle House.) The wheels looked like someone sledgehammered them, and the tires were as bald as the surface of the moon. Duct tape and Bondo made appearances from bumper to bumper, making it look like an army tank drawn on construction paper by a six-year-old. John installed wooden racks on either side of the bed to better equip it for his chosen profession: junk hauling.

One could never guess what John had in the bed of that truck when he pulled up to get gas. The motor from a 1984 Firebird. Five broken rocking chairs and a tractor tire. Twenty-five sets of rims for a Cadillac Seville. An assortment of taxidermy collected from an evicted trailer or house. I asked him about it, and the reply was always the same: "Just some sheeyat I run across out and about."

You could hear John coming from miles away. The truck's muffler was ripped off in a pasture some years before, and John never bothered to replace it. When it was full of junk, the engine whined louder than CNN would if President Bush was caught jaywalking in Crawford, Texas. The truck spewed oil and antifreeze with such regularity that I had a quart of Castrol 10W-30 waiting for him.

Pumping gas into this jalopy was impossible. I had to hold the pump handle sideways at about eight o'clock and insert the nozzle only about a quarter of the way into the line. I could pump only ten cents at a time at a snail's pace, or the truck would regurgitate with such force that I'd become a walking matchstick if I stood close enough to get sprayed. It took twenty minutes to pump five dollars. John would have time to buy his beer, Funyuns, and Marlboros and to smoke two cigarettes before I was done. He would soak in the admiration of the old-timers that valued a man who got the most out of his vehicle.

He would thank me for pumping gas into "the purtiest truck in Cassville" before choking us all to death on exhaust as he pulled away. Larry would remark, "I wonder how much he would take for that truck?" The other bench dwellers would chime in of course.

"I saw him hauling a tool shed on that thing one day."

"John tied a rope to a grain silo and pulled it down with that truck."

"I bet he won't git on it."

We would not have had it any other way.

CHAPTER 16

Lapsed Baptists and "Natcher Laaght"

BEER THIRTY.

Miller time.

It's five o'clock somewhere.

Let me get six Schlitzes.

We have all heard these phrases when people are ready to hit the bottle wide open. At happy hours, frat parties, tailgates, or just hanging out for an excuse to imbibe, it really does not matter. Drinkers are all the same at the end of the day. People have a certain look when they are hell bent for leather when it comes to alcohol.

Men of this generation have an extra pep in their step and a Cheshire grin when they get near the liquor store. The tie is loosened and the shirt is untucked, ready to make war on the liver and cognitive abilities for the next six to eight hours. Men will let the cashier know just how drunk they plan to get. They utter things like "Tonight is going to be epic," and many now follow it up with a social media postings about how "redonk" the night is going to be.

Older generations of men did not brag about their level of drunkenness or the events of the night before. They just popped a Goody powder, drank a coffee, and moved on.

Women are slightly more sheepish in public, but that is only a ruse. They wait until they get into the car with their friends before holding up the bottle and yelling "giiiiiiirlllls niiiight!" Everyone in the car must respond in kind and then post on social media with the bottle of rosé next to their faces with a silly quote like "my BFF for the night #fourhottiesandabottle." Whatever happened to the classy, martini-drinking females of the 1940s, with their cigarette holders and pearl necklaces?

In Cassville, we had all types of drinkers.

FULL-BLOWN ALCOHOLICS: THE CASES BEYOND REPAIR

These folks drank anything, anytime. Many of them were functioning and were not bad folks—they just could not stay away from the sauce.

People like George, who waited for us to open the doors at 6:00 a.m., shaking uncontrollably from DTs because, unfortunately, he couldn't drink in his sleep. He had to kill a twenty-two-ounce Budweiser before he could pay us, because the shakes were so violent.

There was Clayton, who ran out of disability money on Friday night after buying quarts of Budweiser all week. He scrounged up enough change to buy rubbing alcohol and orange juice.

Junior, from the trailer park, had teeth the color of road tar, wore the same shirt every day, and took a shower once every vernal equinox. Dad had the Lysol ready when Junior walked in the door. He would drink no less than a case of Busch in a day, and he once pissed his pants while he was paying us, right in front of his ten-year-old son.

Sandy bought mouthwash every weekend because her "husband's relatives from Texas were in town and forgot to bring some with them." I guessed those Texans loved visiting Cassville and brushing their teeth. I never saw Sandy sober, even in the early morning hours.

Day Drinkers

These drinkers were retired, disabled, or too lazy to work but found the time to hit the bottle all day.

They always bought single beers and returned numerous times throughout the day, resulting in a drunken progression that was fun to watch. They went from happy-go-lucky personalities to annoyingly chatty to unbelievably crass to a colossal state of depression to a stumbling, slurring disaster between 9:00 a.m. and 5:00 p.m.

Dwight was a black man who lived about a mile from the store. He worked for the Postal Service for years until he was injured by a wayward vehicle, leaving him mentally and physically disabled. Dwight could walk and talk, but often, his words were nonsense like "Hey, man, I seen two ducks fightin' a rabbit down at Tennessee Screet." He had a salt-and-pepper beard, was wire thin, and wore a mismatched shirt and tie ensemble every day, with high tops and slacks.

Dwight bought six Olde English 800 quarts per day—the first two before lunch. He would ride his bike up from Rudy

York Road. Dwight always had a plastic bag full of newspapers or *TV Guide* magazines hanging on the handlebars, where he would stuff the quarts of beer and haul ass to the house.

The third and fourth beers would come between 1:00 and 3:00 p.m. This time, Dwight walked, as he did not want to wreck his bike into one of the many perilous ditches on Cassville Road. He still had the plastic bag, in his hands this time, and his gibberish took on a new life: "I gotta frame a Jeep to my skullcap. Hey, man, for real this time. Gahhhhh."

The fifth and sixth beers would be obtained between 5:00 and 7:00 p.m. Dwight would be riding shotgun in his brother Darrell's Caprice this time, still with the plastic bag. Darrell always called me "Easy Money" and would say, "Gotta get this fool his beer. You know how he be." Dwight's eyes would be bugged, out and he would be stumbling in the door. "Sistas be like, naw, man. Uggghhhhhh. Hey! Shake dat. No. OK. OOOOOKKKKK!"

Lapsed Baptists
They pulled up to the door at random times, like 2:37 p.m., and want you to hand the beer to them in a bag. Appearances had to be kept up.

After-Work Power Drinkers
The crowd of construction workers, road crews, brick masons, city or county workers, and plumbers or electricians would pile in around 5:30 p.m. These were the Dwaynes, Rickys, Billys, and Bobbys of the world, and they only wanted three things—beer in suitcases, cigarettes, and bags of ice. There was no hesitation

on their part, and I knew that entire case would be destroyed by midnight. I knew because they would come back in the morning buying Goody powders and coffee, mumbling "Godalmighty" with ten-pound eyelids.

Mexican Males
Marlboro and Budweiser ought to write these guys a thank-you card. A group of five or more would come in at the same time as the after-work power drinkers because they worked on the same job site. Each one would get two packs of Marlboro Reds and enough beer to plaster the starting offensive line of the Atlanta Falcons. Most of them were not even five foot six, 150 pounds, and they would polish off every one of those beers. Strangely, they never seemed hungover in the mornings.

The Six-Pack Crowd
These were middle-aged guys with children, and they were hanging on to their adolescence by way of Coors Light. They worked "in town" (a.k.a. Cartersville) and wore Polo shirts and loafers to work. They might have had associate degrees or actually graduated from colleges, which was evidenced by their lighthearted campus vernacular in reference to Milwaukee's Best ("Beast") and Natural Light (Natty). The power drinkers scoffed at this amateurism: it was "Mwkee's Bess" and "Natcher Laaaght."

Reminiscent Sober Seniors
These were men who used to drink heavily in their youth until they quit for health, marital, or legal reasons. These guys drank

hard whiskey, went to bars where you "could get knifed for looking sideways," and always knew somebody tougher than anyone you knew. Many of them sat out on the benches and told stories of inebriation from the 1940s to '70s that always ended with them in jail, in the hospital, broke, or sleeping on the couch

The oldest plumber in town was Earl, who wore overalls every single day of his life. He was also drunk for forty straight years, according to his own word and the word of 99 percent of the people who knew him back then. Larry always confirmed Earl's tales with a stream of tobacco spit and a hearty "boy, Earl ain't kiddin' around. Pickled all damn day."

When I asked, "Good God, Earl, what about the hangovers?" He said, "Hell, I wudn't never hungover. I never sobered up." Earl apparently woke up and drank two beers at 3:00 a.m. to keep the party going into the next day. There were stories of him passing out under people's sinks or falling asleep in his truck during lunch and pissing himself.

Another story earned Earl legendary status. According to those in the know, back in the '60s, Earl was called upon to help the pastor of his church tar the roof of his home on a hot summer day. Earl, being a good Christian, obliged and went to the pastor's home free of charge. However, Earl being Earl, he did not leave his home without a stocked cooler.

The heat was beating down, and the pastor got thirsty after a couple of hours of hard labor. He was ill prepared and asked Earl, who was half in the bag, if he had any water. Unfortunately for the man of the cloth, Earl only had Schlitz. It took a few minutes of convincing, but the pastor finally relented and quenched

Brad Stephens

his thirst on the sweet nectar of Milwaukee, Wisconsin. Being a lightweight and nondrinker, three Schlitzes led to the drunk pastor falling off the roof and landing in his holly bushes, cutting himself all to pieces.

Three of the older guys (JT, Jimmy, and Willie) on the benches had been friends for years and told a story about being so drunk one night in Aragon, Georgia, that they decided to drive down to Steinhatchee, Florida, to go deep-sea fishing. After batting it around, JT and Jimmy decided that their wives would not appreciate them disappearing in the middle of the night to Florida.

Unfortunately for them, the one who did not adhere to this better course of action was Willie, the driver of their vehicle. On the way home, the other two passed out, and Willie got on 41 going south. JT and Jimmy came to right outside of Valdosta, Georgia—295 miles south of Cassville. Willie cackled as they crossed the Florida line to get a day of fishing done in the gulf.

CHAPTER 17

Yoda

THE SUN BEAT DOWN ON the pavement on a hot summer day in 1994. It was one of those days it was so hot the birds weren't even flying around. I was back in the hardware arranging the cracked corn and scratch feed, pricing the bags, and separating them according to their sizes. I didn't mind that kind of work, honestly. I always felt like I accomplished something when I put up two hundred bags of feed, soil, peat moss, and fertilizer. Not to mention twenty-five blocks of salt for deer season, which weighed fifty pounds, but I swore to everything holy that they weighed two hundred pounds apiece. (You ever tried to carry one? It's more awkward than watching *Boogie Nights* with your parents.)

Anyhow, I was tossing bags left and right, when Rusty yelled, "Got one on the front!" I put down my price gun and sprinted down the first aisle, past the cereal, the paper towels, and the medicine. The heat wave just blasted my thirteen-year-old face. There was not a breeze within a hundred miles of us. The vehicle parked beside the gas pumps was a common sight for my eyes. A mid-1980s Camaro with a hatch, primer gray, missing muffler, leaking oil, and shaking to a stop next to the regular unleaded pump. The hood was being held down with a twisted coat hanger. There are dead wasps (wawstes, remember?) under the glass in the hatch. The driver door opened with a creak, and this man stepped out. At least, I thought it was a man.

It weighed about a hundred pounds soaking wet, with a sunken face and missing teeth. Its arms were down to its knees, and it was wearing a tattered flannel shirt, pants, boots, and a cap that read, "This cap is mine. Everything else is hers." He muttered in English, "Gimme two dollars' worf" (two dollars' worth of gas). Back then, two dollars could get you to Marietta and back. (Now, you might be able to get from the store to Firetower Road before you have to use your finger. [Alan Jackson reference +1].)

The man strode into the store. I unhooked the pump and turned the knob to clear the machine for pumping. Our pumps did not have credit card capability. The pumps were older than me, my brother, and Rusty combined. That was part of the charm—the hum of that tiny motor inside the pump. Plus, it was funny to watch people from Atlanta try to figure out how they worked.

Genius number one: "My gosh, Bill, where does the card go? I can't turn this on!"

Genius number two: "I don't know! Excuse me, young man!" (addressing me).

Me (turning the knob for them): "Y'all gotta pay inside, and we don't take Discover."

I opened the gas tank door. There was a napkin in the place of a cap. I was sure the cap was stolen when the last person siphoned gas out of this tank. That was a common occurrence back then, strangely. I started the pump and watched the cents tick by on the meter. I stared down at my Air Jordans, covered in dirt and 10-10-10 fertilizer. Neen was gonna kill me for working in my new shoes—I just knew it. Suddenly, the passenger door popped open, startling me. The vehicle rocked, like somebody was getting momentum to throw themselves out of the seat and into the parking lot.

A figure materialized.

It was much shorter than the man, probably five foot and hunched over. It had dirty yellow/white/gray hair matted down on its head. It was wearing a housecoat that appeared to have been pink at some point. Now, it was brown/yellow/gray with pink spots. Waddling around the car, it glanced over at me. Making eye contact with it, I was taken aback.

Now, we had been subject to many strange-looking people, servicing the area that we did. However, this one was especially heinous. One eye was closed, and the other was opened, staring at me. The face was wrinkled beyond belief, and the chin had stringy white hairs growing out of it. The mouth was slightly opened, revealing brown tobacco-stained teeth. The brown tobacco juice had made its way onto the chin and the cheeks. The sight of this figure made me forget how much I wanted a hot dog for lunch.

The figure was a woman, I assumed, since the man's cap said "everything else is hers." I guess this was "her." I was so busy staring at her that I messed up and pumped $3.25 into their tank. Sweet. That was a $1.25 out of my pay and a free trip to

Chattanooga for them. I was about to stop the pump and grab the napkin (cap). For some reason, I kept hearing this clicking noise. I look around for the source. I looked under the car. I put my ear up to the pump. Maybe the belt was loose. Nope. My ears finally zoned in on what it was.

I cast my eyes toward it.

There were a few regrets in my life...I never studied abroad, I never saw Michael Jordan play live, and I once accused a friend of stealing my wallet before I found it in my shorts in the laundry. None of these unfortunate events compared to what my eyes saw that day. The woman was barefoot. The clicking was a long black toenail, on her left foot, striking the pavement with each step. It had to be two inches long.

I closed my eyes, nauseated. "God, please don't let me hurl."

Into the store I went, following behind her. The smell hit my nose. A combination of body odor, urine, feces, and tobacco. That explained the coloration on the housecoat. I clenched my jaws, resisting the Waffle House hash browns that were itching to escape my stomach.

Rusty mouthed, "Holy hell." He grabbed the Lysol under the cabinet. She waddled past the candy rack, click, click, click.

The smell was permeating the air, destroying the sweet BBQ scent that was wafting among the aisles. She came to a stop at the ice cream cooler. This indicated that she wanted one of us to dip an ice cream for her. Rusty looked at me, looked back at the hardware, and shouted to no one, "Be right there, sir!" He ran away laughing. I was stuck. There was no joy in Mudville.

I opened the cooler door, and in the best tone I could muster, said, "What would you like?" The woman looked up at me, one eye still closed, chin whiskers waving in the air conditioning, and said, "Gimme a dip a 'niller" (a dip of vanilla).

That was the fastest ice cream ever dipped. That vanilla was frozen solid, and I had skinny arms, but I could have smashed clear to the bottom of that three-gallon Mayfield tub. I wanted her gone. I handed her the cone. With the tobacco still in her mouth, she began to lick the ice cream. It got in her chin whiskers. I saw Rusty watching from the back, aghast. My gag reflex was working overtime. The man was standing at the counter, ready to pay me. He got a pack of cigarettes and a can of Bruton snuff for his woman and handed me the cash. Click, click, click. She exited the building. He left with a "'preciate it," and out to the chariot he walked.

Rusty was weaving through the aisles, uttering every four-letter word in the book, dousing the air with "country flowers" or "summer rain" or whatever scent we could find to annihilate the foulness left behind. I heard the Camaro rev up, and it departed in a cloud of smoke and dust.

For years, when we saw that Camaro pull up, a collective groan would arise. Neen would go hide in the walk-in cooler. Larry would get in his truck and head home. Out would come the Lysol, and our eyes would avert to the ceiling because the woman never wore shoes, so the click, click, click happened each and every time she came in. So did the housecoat, the closed eye, the smell, and the chin whiskers. She got an ice cream every time, always vanilla. (Even now, the thought of that incomparable disgustingness destroys my appetite.) We never knew her name, but we bestowed "Yoda" upon her because it was the closest related creature we could think of to describe her.

The legend of Yoda grew every time she entered the store, kind of like a big fish that got bigger every time the story was told. We did figure out a couple of things about her. She lived with about twelve other people in a shack up in Adairsville. Her supposed granddaughters, who were two of the twelve, worked at a local restaurant, so any trips to that particular establishment were absolutely out of the question. Mom saw them working in the drive-thru after we ordered dinner and she promptly tossed all four of our burgers in the trash. I wouldn't buy a cup of ice from that place, even now.

CHAPTER 18

Never Judge a Man Covered in Roofing Tar

DOES ANYONE ELSE LOVE THE smell of Pine Sol?

That scent always signified closing time at Cass Grocery because that was what we used to mop the floors at the end of the day. I would push the bucket full of water along the aisles, soaking the tiles with steaming water mixed with Pine Sol. I would just inhale that wonderful concoction and watch Dad clean the deli slicer. He never mopped floors once we got old enough to do so. I think cleaning the slicer was his happy place.

We kept the place as clean as possible. It was tough though, as many of our customers were construction workers, DOT road-crew members, farmers, and self-employed landscapers—people who were filthy ten hours a day and dragged that filth across our floors after quitting time. I did not care much, as those people were *our* people. The lifeblood of Cassville.

I always enjoyed Ray, who worked on a roofing crew all over the county.

Ray was in his midfifties and weighed about 140 pounds soaking wet. He wore a flannel shirt and Dickies pants and boots that appeared to be three sizes too big. The only time I did not see Ray covered in tar and dirt was at 6:00 a.m. before work and on Sundays. His hands were like sandpaper, his skin was like leather, and he smelled like a gym bag that was left in a hot truck for a week. Such was life for a roofing man.

His best friend Tommy was no different. They worked in the same crew and ran in the same circles. Tommy's idea of fun was a twenty-four pack of Milwaukee's Best, fixing busted car engines and signing up for toughman competitions across north Georgia. I don't know if he ever won any of those fights, but betting against Cassville men in any sort of combat is not a good idea.

No matter what was going on, Ray would walk in the door with a "How y'all doin', boys?" Despite his rough appearance, he was a model citizen. He never wrote a bad check, never complained about prices, never stole anything, and never asked for favors. If he bought anything on credit, on payday Ray would immediately leave the bank with his cashed paycheck and reimburse us. Larry often remarked what a "good ol' boy" Ray was.

I was pretty sure Ray was raised in Ball Ground or somewhere in Cherokee County, but he was a Cassville man through and through. He and his wife lived in a rough trailer park, where people went to jail almost daily for domestic violence, dealing drugs, petty theft, and probation violations. Despite those harrowing surroundings, you never heard a peep out of Ray. In fact, most of the crazy drunks, violent criminals, and schizophrenic meth-heads seemed to chill out around him.

I learned a valuable lesson through Ray one day.

The girl I was dating came to visit me at work one weekday afternoon. She would often come by and hang around for thirty minutes or so right after school (only if Dad was not around, of course). On this particular day, she came in an hour later than usual and was propped up next to me at the cash register around 5:00 p.m.

At Cass Grocery, it was amazing the difference an hour made. The store at 4:00 p.m. was chaotic during the school year. The county system had three schools within a two-mile radius of us, and the store was a school bus stop for many kids. Candy and ice cream jumped off the shelves faster than a Daytona 500 ticket giveaway at the Waffle House. Two or three high schoolers would beg me to sell them cigarettes. Stressed-out mothers would be screaming, "Y'all hurry up. I ain't *got* all *day*!" (In reality, she sat on the couch watching game shows and soap operas until school ended, and she wanted to get back to catch Maury's latest DNA test.)

The store at 5:00 p.m. was drastically different. You could not find a person under eighteen anywhere—it was the just-got-off-work crowd. People looking relieved, happy, stressed, depressed, worked over, or worked up. Candy and ice cream sales were replaced by milk, bread, headache powders, beer, and cigarettes. Half of the gas customers would cruise in on fumes every day, with the same remark, "Maybe I oughta get more than two dollars' worth every time." People looked for credit to get a few things until payday. The stressed-out mothers would return at 5:00 p.m. to get some beer after watching

Maury tell D'Shawndray that he was not the father of three-month-old L'Eritrea.

With Ray, "quittin' time" took on another meaning. Working on somebody's roof all day, bent over and sweating, covered in filth—not really ideal when you lived in a trailer park with no education—yet he always had a smile on his face. I guess he was just happy to have a job. He felt like he earned his keep and seemed really happy as he took his long strides in those oversized boots through our door.

"How y'all doin, boys," he said as he made his way to the beer cooler. As he passed by, the wind from his entrance wafted across the floor and infiltrated my girlfriend's delicate nasal passages. I was used to that smell. Sweat, dirt, tar, body odor, and cigarettes were not exactly a recipe for the next Ralph Lauren fragrance, but it was Ray—I couldn't have cared less about his smell or appearance, which was especially disheveled on this day.

My girlfriend made a face like Ray had just announced his allegiance to Hitler.

"Where y'all go today?" I asked Ray.

"Aw, hell, we was all over Darsvull [Adairsville] today, boy. I am *whupped*," Ray replied as he walked toward us with his twelve pack of Natural Light. His hair was matted down, his hands were black, and his face was weathered from the sun—but it was Ray.

"Gimme two packs of mah cig-ritts, please," he said as he dug his wallet out of his back pocket. He was a loyal smoker of Basic cigarettes, the cheap stuff. "They'll all kill ya," Ray said.

As he dug in his wallet, I felt a nudge on my side. My girlfriend mouthed "oh my God" and put her hand over her nose. I gave her a terse "stop" look and shoved her hand away. He handed me a wad of damp cash from his pocket, and I gave him some change back. He told me to keep ten dollars of it because he owed my dad some money from a couple of days ago. "Your daddy let Rhonda get some things on credit. Tell him I 'preciate it."

After I bagged Ray's things and he left, my girlfriend launched into a tirade of how disgusting Ray was. How the lack of attention to appearance and lack of education bred people like him. If he cared a little more, he could get ahead in life...blah, blah, blah. It was then I realized that judging people by their looks was what was disgusting. While I'd admit Ray was not a picture of cleanliness, decorum, or monetary success—he was a good man with a good heart. I preferred him over many people who had those other three attributes.

It was people like Ray who paid our bills and kept our business going. The rough people, the manual laborers, the beer drinkers, and the hell-raisers. Our most loyal customers were often the people covered in crap and weathered by the elements or unfortunate life choices. I could only appreciate them and defend Ray's honor from someone who had no clue what he was about.

I dumped her soon thereafter. There were three things you did not mess with—Cassville people, the Georgia Bulldogs, and the Waffle House. Everything else was fair game.

CHAPTER 19

Your Life Is Not Complete until You Have Survived a Point-Blank .22 Shot to the Head

"WELL, YOU KNOW, THEY FROM the trailer park..."

That was the explanation given for the hijinks of many of our customers over the years, often accompanied by raised eyebrows and a hint of condescension. It was almost as if that statement justified them—that living in a community of modular homes just lent itself to suspect behavior.

You stole a 1986 Camaro, took a joyride to Adairsville, and totaled it in a ditch on Pleasant Valley Road? You got caught with enough meth to kill an elephant, ditched your van at a roadblock, and made a run for it into the woods? You slapped a teacher on a field trip and threatened him with a concealed switchblade? You had to go to the hospital because you punched your wife's boyfriend's driver's-side window out and he caught your arm and dragged you down Cassville Road? You only needed one explanation—"the trailer park."

"The trailer park" could be a number of places in Cassville. There were at least four within walking distance of the store, and all of them were full of drug addicts, thieves, juvenile delinquents, and mothers who wore shoes only when the pavement was too hot to walk on. My wife, who was raised in suburban Atlanta, had never seen a trailer park until she visited Cassville for the first time.

"Oh, so those are real? I thought you were talking about KOA campgrounds."

The land of airbrushed T-shirts, immobilized vehicles, restraining orders, and emergency-room visits. The inspiration for the Family Violence Act, the destination for disability checks, and deputy sheriffs answering the twenty-seven[th] call about noise violations from the trailer with a fan in the window. Where at least one adult family member rode a bicycle full time, wives were "old ladies," and the men owned mesh-back hats with sayings like "Kiss my rebel ass." A cornucopia of dissonance, destruction and debauchery...oh, how I loved it.

When the local paper decided to start posting the police blotter from the previous day, it created a whole new chain of gossip—and you could bet your paycheck that somebody from one of those four addresses would be on the list. After they would be released, they would walk proudly through our door—"You seen me in the paper? It took three of 'em to get me in the car." It was a source of pride to be dragged screaming and cussing into the back of a police car. Going down swinging was a badge of honor, and these folks never went quietly.

One such man shot his old lady at point-blank range with a .22 pistol while she slept. Apparently, he suspected her of cheating and decided, in a drunken stupor, to kill her. To that point, the biggest accomplishment in their lives was getting Willie Nelson's autograph in the Waffle House outside of Heflin, Alabama. Rather than splitting through her skull and killing her instantly, the bullet deflected and passed over her eyebrow, exiting harmlessly, with only four stitches needed. So now, she had Willie's autograph and had survived a head shot. After he got out of prison for attempted murder, he moved right back in with her, and they stayed married until she passed away from a drug overdose ten years later.

Another man was arrested for attempted murder when he tried to kill his son with a hatchet. He was high on meth and thought his son was a ghost, so naturally he grabs a hatchet and starts swinging wildly. Weeks later, their neighbor's son was hit by an F-150 on his bicycle while he was running from a store he just ripped off. He did not die, but the two cartons of Winstons he lifted from the shelf were crushed and he went to jail.

With many of the common-law marriages still thriving and the fact that all of these people would claim a fifth cousin, their trailers were open crash pads for any wayward family members or friends. I had met several "cousin's ex-boyfriend" and "my stepson's uncle by marriage" hanging around for months at a time.

People on the run from the law in another county. Kicked out by their own old lady. Evicted and homeless or just plain sorry and listless—it did not matter. I noticed a sadness about many of them, as if they sometimes looked in the mirror and regretted their life choices. Many of them had a constant air of uncertainty and stress, probably from closets full of skeletons and a lifetime of wandering.

The revolving door never stopped moving, bringing in more people who kept Marlboro, Budweiser, and Mountain Dew flying off the shelves like F-14s off an aircraft carrier. Of course, they would screw up by stealing from their own people or trying to sleep with someone in the house, or they'd start a fire while smoking in bed, and boom—out they'd go.

Neen decided to rent a house near one of these trailer parks. Normally, this would be worrisome but Larry and his wife lived next door. If anyone messed with Neen, Larry would kill them. Despite their rough nature and general nonchalance about the law, these folks did not fool around with Larry. People would talk tough about defending themselves, but Larry let his actions doing all the talking. I knew Neen was safe.

She was outside pruning her brushes one day, when she was approached by one of its residents, Leon, who knew her from the soup kitchen at the local church. Leon was a twentysomething white guy who always wore NASCAR gear and never worked a day in his life. He gave her a sob story about his baby needing milk and being short on cash. Neen was normally skeptical, but she could not stand the thought of a starving child. She agreed to give him five dollars, and he walked to the store after thanking her profusely.

Leon was the quintessential resident of this trailer park. Neen's scanner probably broadcast at least three of his arrests for disorderly conduct or public drunkenness. He had an internal magnet that drew him to alcohol, fistfights, and poor decisions. This fool tried to give himself a tattoo of Dale Earnhardt's "3" on his right bicep, but he'd looked in the mirror as he jabbed the ink into his pale skin. So when the finished product was unveiled, it was backward. To his credit, Leon went shirtless most of the time to display his homage to the Intimidator.

Twenty minutes after Neen's loan, Leon tried to sneak by with a single paper bag in the telltale shape of a forty-ounce Olde English 800 bottle. Too bad for him that Neen *always* had an eye on the road. Neen pranced right up to him with hands on her hips, looked him right in the eye, and, with an admonishing tone, said, "Boy, I hope you enjoy that beer. Give me my change. Don't you *never* ask me for another dime."

All Leon could say was, "Yes, Miss Nancy. I'm sorry."

SEX, DRUGS, AND STEVIE RAY VAUGHAN

The Wehunt family moved into the trailer park in the late '90s from LaGrange, Georgia. I had no idea what brought them to Cassville, as the husband, Randy, was disabled, and the wife, Kim, worked part time at a truck stop. I was quite certain Troup County had plenty of truck stops for her and trailers for a pill-popping loafer like Randy.

As nefarious family members materialized over the years, the Wehunts graduated into meth usage and slid down the hill of addiction. Teeth and weight fell off both of them like bark from a pine tree. He would dart into the store and walk in circles, sweating profusely and loading up on candy bars. Randy once tried to steal twenty-five Dixie Outfitters T-shirts from us and then cried on his knees in the parking lot after Matt caught him, professing his love for us.

"Man, I love y'all, man! I'm all f****ed up! Don't call the law on me, man! I love you!"

We did not call the law. He went home and stayed away for a few weeks.

I gave Randy credit for one thing—the man could play guitar quite well. One afternoon, he pulled into the parking lot in his step-side Chevy pickup and popped his tailgate, eyes bugging out and licking his lips like a starved dog in a slaughterhouse. Decked out in his finest cutoff Big Johnson shirt and a cowboy hat, Randy maneuvered himself into position on his tailgate.

He plugged in an amplifier out by the ice machine and began to wail away on his electric guitar, playing such songs as Stevie Ray Vaughan's "Crossfire" and "Voodoo Chile." He had a good crowd of people gather around, and between songs he would tweak out, take a pull of Mountain Dew, and keep on playing. For the free entertainment, we gave him a six-pack of Natural Light.

One morning, a neighbor came in the store with a grim look on his face and explained that Randy passed away the night before. Randy and Kim had hosted a "get-together" in their double-wide, where every person was smacked out on pills and meth for twenty-four hours. At some point, Randy had ingested too much and became severely ill. He sat down in his recliner and died of a heart attack while his partygoers continued on. According to the police who worked the scene, it took the partyers four hours to realize that Randy was dead.

A steady stream of people from the trailer park made their way to the store, trying to get the lowdown on Randy's death. Many of them proclaimed their disbelief that meth-ridden, toothless, sore-covered Randy was indeed gone to the afterlife. One man said, "You can say what you want—you could count on Randy."

Yes, you could count on Randy actually. Every single time he walked through our door, somebody inevitably would ask, "What the hell is the matter with that dude?" Legend had it that Randy died flashing peace signs on both hands. I think he was counting the number of pills he had left.

Their kids were sneaky little goblins who would steal anything from fish hooks to motor oil. We had a blue cardboard bin of cheap cigarettes that sat by the front counter, and I could not count how many times some scraggly-haired ten-year-old in a Big Johnson T-shirt tried to swipe a $1.19 pack of GPC Lights. As drugged up and crazy as their parents were, when I told them about attempted theft, these folks would tan the child's hide right there in the parking lot (probably because they told them to steal menthols).

"You Can't Win if You Don't Play"

Despite their lack of fiscal means, these people could not resist playing the lottery. It had a tractor beam that would lock them in and draw them right to the counter. The scratch-off tickets were like a pile of manure, and these folks were the swarms of horse-flies buzzing over it. These were people who ate Fudge Rounds for breakfast but would blow twenty-five dollars Lucky 7's lottery tickets.

"Today's the day," said Wendell, a regular player. Wendell worked for a paving company until he developed carpal tunnel syndrome and started drawing disability. Every Friday, he would drive up in his Chevy S-10 with a mismatched camper shell and busted transmission. It could only get to third gear, so you could hear the screaming engine coming down Cassville Road at thirty-seven miles per hour.

Wendell would cash his disability check, go home to hit the meth pipe, and then drive up to us. By the time he walked through the door, he would be sweating gravy and pacing circles in the floor. He would instantly order fifty dollars' worth of one-dollar scratch-off tickets and start scratching with his lucky nickel.

The meth coursing through his body would go into overdrive, and he would have to back up, scratch his forearms profusely, and groan loudly. After winning ten dollars, he would continue to throw down the cash. Matt and I would just stare as this man would annihilate his disability check in twenty minutes and completely lose control of his bodily functions twice during that time.

By the time Wendell was through, he would only have enough money left to buy Funyuns, some Reese's Pieces, and a forty-ounce Bud Ice.

"Man, I told you today was the day. This Bud Ice will last me all night."

CHAPTER 20

If You See a Cutoff Def Leppard T-Shirt, You Better Run

TROUBLE COMES IN ALL FORMS in life—it is an inevitable occurrence for all of us. What differentiates people is the kind of trouble and how they handle it. Some people have money trouble. When you take out three mortgages, finance two trucks, two four-wheelers, a time-share in Panama City Beach, and an above-ground pool based on your overtime pay, you are asking for trouble. Just like most marriages and anyone playing for the Miami Marlins—overtime ain't gonna last.

Others have marriage troubles. If a man's common-law wife is running around with his cousin and then takes his debit card and cleans him out at Hobby Lobby—yeah, there may be a disagreement there.

Kids seemed to cause more strife than joy, and based on my experience, troubled Cassville couples would wage war right in front of everyone at the store over it. Troy and Wanda would have a knock-down, drag out over whether little Cody Ray could have a seventy-nine-cent Milky Way and a Yoo-hoo for breakfast. Everyone knew this was the breakfast of champions, Wanda.

Then you had legal trouble, which was a small-town specialty. We had enough riffraff, scalawags, rednecks, drug addicts, and mischief to fill a police blotter nightly. It was not even a shock to most people to learn of a fistfight, a meth bust, gunfire, or anything burning to ashes in a suspicious fiery inferno.

All people wanted to know was who it was and when it happened—they knew the subjects of this brouhaha did not die. You could not kill these people. A hydrogen bomb could explode a hundred yards from their trailer, and they would emerge, wandering around with the surviving cockroaches and aerial bacteria, asking "What the hayul?"

These were the kind of people who showed up at random times of the day and said ominous things.

"Hey, man, come look in the back of my truck." (The possibilities were endless here—deer or snake carcasses, stolen property, and firearms were the usual suspects.)

"You seen my wife today?"

"Do y'all still sell ten-gauge shells?"

"Does kerosene burn slower than gas?"

Detecting trouble was no problem in Cassville. People wore it like a badge and waved it like a flag most of the time. Trouble was brewing in Cassville if

* a sixteen-year-old kid covered in tattoos traded a ten-dollar bill for a roll of quarters;

* a drunk neighbor came in the store with nothing on but jean shorts and a mesh-back hat that simply said "Rebel," asking where the chainsaw files were;
* a 1987 Buick Regal flew through the parking lot and screeched to a halt, followed by a 1983 Firebird with no muffler;
* a man nicknamed "Mule" walked in the door and said, "Y'all hear what happened to me last night?"; and
* a male in a cutoff Def Leppard T-shirt was on the pay-phone at 3:00 a.m., and his female companion was lying on the hood of his Mustang.

OK, those did not seem so harmful at first glance. However, if you hailed from the 30123, you knew that none of these scenarios were going to work out well. I knew this from personal experience.

The sixteen-year-old kid, Jackie, was a classmate of mine in school. He traded the ten-dollar bill for a roll of quarters at 7:00 a.m., which was the opposite of what usually happened. Cassville people loved to gather all their loose change and cash it in with us. It was like Christmas morning when they would come in with a Ziploc bag full of rolled change—they would instantly use the cash to buy beer and lottery tickets.

I remember thinking how odd it was that Jackie wanted a roll of quarters instead. He had no car to wash, and there was no arcade within thirty-five miles. I thought maybe it was for the vending machine at school, but since he only went once a week, that was out of the question.

About two hours later, with the roll of quarters taped inside his fist, Jackie approached another classmate, Sammy, at his locker.

"I know you been seein' Jessica, you piece of..."

The punch landed, and that sickening crunch of broken bones reverberated off the walls of the hallway. Sammy lost seven teeth, suffered a broken jaw, and had to have reconstructive surgery to fix his disfigured face. While Sammy lay in a heap on the ground, Jackie laughed and spit on him. If you were going to see someone's ex-girlfriend in Cassville, you'd better clear it with the former boyfriend first, especially one who got his first tattoo at age fourteen and was on a first-name basis with every cop and drug dealer in the county.

Jackie was arrested, expelled from school, and started dealing drugs full time. He would hang around the benches, usually shirtless, with flips-flops, socks, and sweatpants. Somehow, he was able to store a .38 Special in those sweatpants, which he pointed at one of his friends in the store after an argument over whose turn it was to buy cigarettes.

The drunk neighbor was a man named Donnie. He wanted a chainsaw file to sharpen his chainsaw blade so he could saw a giant oak tree down in his front yard. It was all over his power lines, and he was worried about it, but Georgia Power refused to take action. So what did Donnie do?

He threw a party, and a dozen of his closest friends showed up with cases of Natural Light on Saturday morning. They drank all day to get up the nerve to take this tree down. This oak was enormous, one of those types of trees that lined the property of

Tara in *Gone with the Wind*. Except this was no Tara. It was a block house with two nonoperating Mustangs out front and a mutt called Poncho chained to a piece of buried rebar.

Donnie and friends descended on this tree about two o'clock and start sawing. Fueled by Natural Light, dulled senses, and adrenaline from defiance, these rednecks were like a squad of marines assaulting a fixed position. After about two hours into the operation, with a chorus of Ric Flair "wooooos," the oak bobbed and weaved and crashed down...on the power lines and completely blocked Cassville Road. Georgia Power ended up dealing with the tree after all. Donnie was arrested, and we lost power for the rest of the day—all of the milk spoiled and the Bud Light in the beer cooler got warm, to the dismay of all those stocking up for Sunday. 'Preciated that, Donnie.

The 1987 Buick Regal was occupied by Ricky and Tonya, who was Ricky's girlfriend of about two years. The 1983 Firebird was occupied by Kristy, Ricky's wife of twelve years. Kristy jumped out of the Firebird, calling Tonya everything but white and brandishing a baseball bat. Like a surgeon, she went to work on Ricky's car—the headlights, the taillights, the quarter panels, the back windshield, the back windows were all destroyed.

She was careful not to hit the front windows or front windshield. She knew that could result in an aggravated battery charge if she hit Ricky or Tonya, who were screaming helplessly during her attack.

"Baby, stop! Baby! Let's talk about this!"

"Oh you wanna talk?! I seen y'all leaving Scott's Motel!"

Kristy finally tired and stopped beating the car. Ricky attempted to get out, but she mustered the strength to raise the bat at him. He jumped back in and speed off. Our parking lot was covered in glass, and Kristy walked up to my dad, who had watched this unfold with his arms crossed. Nothing really shocked Dad anymore.

"Dave, you gonna call the cops on me?" she asked, sobbing.

"No way," Dad replied, handing her a broom and dustpan. "Just clean up the mess." Snitching was not our thing in Cassville.

Mule lived down the road with his wife. Mule worked for the county as an electrician and lived a relatively quiet life. He spent most mornings sitting on the benches—talking about the weather, truck parts, or his latest gun purchase. Mule was one of those men who should not be pushed and would shoot first and ask questions later. He spent deer season in trees, dove season in the fields, rabbit season in the swamp, and duck season in the blind. He was always armed and always ready.

This new face named Jake moved to town, and he was shady. He was crashing with a known meth-dealing family, and he appeared to be breaking the cardinal rule of drug dealing: do not use what you are dealing. He would randomly show up in the middle of the day, buying up all the Swiss Cake Rolls and Three Musketeers bars we had. With wide eyes, neck scratching, and constant sweating and pacing, Jake was a poster child for the effects of meth. He had a habit of wandering around town aimlessly as he came down from his high.

Jake decided to wander into Mule's yard at 3:00 a.m. one night. In his haze, he also thought he could steal Mule's brand-new four-wheeler, even though he was crashing at a house that was in plain sight of Mule's.

Since he was not from Cassville, he was not aware of the other Cassville rules: everyone had an outside dog, and being out past 1:00 a.m. was a no-no. Outside dogs were as common as crab-grass and were better than burglar alarms. If you were out past 1:00 a.m. in Cassville, you were either dealing drugs, stealing something, or going to the Waffle House. Jake was not interested in hash browns that night.

Mule's dog went crazy barking as soon as Jake's flashlight appeared on the four-wheeler's ignition. Seconds later, Mule appeared on his porch in nothing but underwear, and fired a .30-30 round over Jake's head. All of Mule's outside lights turned on. Jake bolted and rans to the woods and tried to circle around to his temporary home, but Mule's dog tracked him all the way and stayed there, barking loudly.

The cops arrived, and Mule puts on a robe and cowboy boots. Jake was taken out of the house and brought to Mule's yard, where he confessed to walking through the yard but not trying to steal the four-wheeler. In his boldness, he asked to press charges against Mule for trying to kill him.

"Boy, if I wanted to kill you, you'd be dead. If I miss, it's on purpose," Mule calmly stated.

The cops laughed at Jake and told Mule, "We'll see you at the huntin' camp on Saturday, right?"

The man in the cutoff Def Leppard T-shirt, and the girl lying on the Mustang, did not do anything that I know of. But if you saw someone on a pay phone at 3:00 a.m. in a town like Cassville, there were only three things that could be going on: a drug deal, arranging for a john to pick you up, or calling your brother to discuss stock trading.

That pay phone was like a black hole of morality—every shady person, every sordid affair, every drug deal, and God knew what else took place on that pay phone. If the police recorded the conversations for a week, The county jail would have had to use the basement to house all the criminals.

These were the days before burner cell phones and fake e-mail addresses, so this pay phone was a gateway for the morally casual Cassville natives to conduct their clandestine business. I worried that it would be vandalized, but I soon realized that these people needed this pay phone. There was no way that some wayward teenager would destroy that phone—it would cut into the profits of certain people who would not have appreciated it.

My dad agreed to have it installed, but I could tell that he worried about the clientele it would bring in. He had good reason to worry. When somebody hung up that phone, immediately walked into the store, and bought shotgun shells or a sledgehammer, he knew an arrest or grievous injury to person or property was about to occur.

One of the more "esteemed" members of our community had a ritual every Sunday afternoon. He was the deacon in a local church and highly thought of by most people. Once he finished lunch with his wife, he would leave his house and park his truck on the south side of the store. He would walk past us on the benches, cross the parking lot, and get on the pay phone.

After a minute of conversation, he would hang up and come in the store to buy a twenty-ounce Coke. He would stand around and talk for about five minutes until he heard the door of his truck slam shut.

"Awright, gotta go," he'd say and scurry out the door. The truck would pull out, and a woman would be sitting in the passenger seat. She lived about a quarter of a mile from the store, and she could not drive because her license was suspended from getting caught with about a pound of cocaine in her Ford Explorer the year before. Her husband was one of the roughest people in town, and if he knew about this, both of them could meet their Maker in about two seconds.

They carried on this affair for years. Everyone suspected it but would not say anything out loud. I guess nobody wanted trouble after all.

CHAPTER 21

Nobody Messed with Mama Kim

MAMA KIM LIVED DOWN THE street from us in a house that my great-grandfather built with his own two hands in the 1920s. I was sure asbestos and lumber were about all that was used to construct this house, but Mama Kim seemed to be just fine.

If you ever wondered, all you had to do was ask.

She was the spriest eighty-five-year-old woman I had ever seen. Mama Kim was short in stature but long in attitude and always put off the don't-mess-with-me vibe—the gruff southern-woman routine: hands on the hips, pursed lips, and a stare that would burn to your very soul. Beneath that exterior, she was a kindhearted, gentle woman who loved all of us very much.

Daddy Kim died from complications related to a stroke in 1982, so I never knew him. I learned from stories told by Neen, Mom, Dad and Larry. Mama Kim and Daddy Kim were married when she was fifteen years old. They went down to the Bartow County Courthouse, said their vows, and returned to their parents' homes.

After a few minutes at the dinner table, Daddy Kim said to his parents, "Well, I married Lucille today."

His mother said, "Well...Dave...go get her!" So, he drove over to Mama Kim's house, picked her up, and they never parted ways until he died.

When my brother and I were too young to work, we had to stay with our grandmothers. I stayed with Neen, and Matt stayed with Mama Kim. I was always welcome at Mama Kim's though, and I would go down there frequently and see her. She had the best lemonade in the history of Georgia, and all you had to do was say "I'm hungr—" and a bowl of chicken and dumplings would suddenly appear before your eyes. This was manna from heaven. This woman did not believe in fat free, sugar free, or watching carbs. Her babies had to eat.

Mama Kim firmly believed that if it was less than seventy degrees outside, you would get pneumonia if you were not wearing a coat. I swore, it would be March, and my poor brother would walk out of her house looking like Ralphie's little brother from *A Christmas Story*. You could push him down, and he would wallow like a turtle on the ground. Nobody dared to complain because nobody messed with Mama Kim.

She kept tabs on us at all times. Mama Kim would call my dad weekly to ask if he paid us for working that week.

"Not yet, Mama Kim. I am going to pay them tonight."

"You better, Dave. I will call DFACS on you. I ain't kiddin'."

She would walk out her door and chastise us for riding my brother's motorcycle too fast, fighting with pine tree branches, throwing rocks from her gravel driveway, or climbing trees that were too high.

"I'm gonna send y'all to Milledgeville!"

This threat was often used by elderly Cassville natives when someone was acting wild and crazy. Milledgeville, Georgia used to be home to more prisons and mental hospitals than anywhere in the United States. If you "ain't right in the head," then you were sent to Milledgeville and never seen again.

Joe loved her because she fed him all her leftovers too, which were always fattening and tasty. She dispelled the myth that chocolate will kill dogs because Joe would eat one of her chocolate pies in two minutes. He probably ate a pie per week for eight years or more and died just after he turned thirteen years old.

One summer day, Matt and I were watching television at her house and drinking lemonade. Suddenly, the movie we were watching turned to snow and remained that way for over an hour. Mama Kim picked up the phone and called the local cable company.

"Yeah, this is Lucille Kimsey. I'm over here on my road, and my cable has been out for an hour. My babies are down here, and they can't watch their programs." Mama Kim had a way of putting things that conveyed annoyance and the risk of possible harm if she did not get her way.

"Uh-huh. Well, I pay for this cable every month. All I watch is the Braves, QVC, and whatever these babies want to see...Now we can't do that. I don't know what I'm paying y'all for. I want five dollars off my bill at the end of the month."

After a few more minutes of negotiating, she hung up. The cable was restored about four hours later, and she turned on the Braves game immediately. Mama Kim was a child of the Depression. Every penny mattered to her. She still hated Herbert Hoover and voted straight Democrat in every election.

Her bill was reduced by five dollars at the end of the month. I knew that would happen, because nobody messed with Mama Kim.

Mama Kim, as with most octogenarians, needed several medications to treat the usual ailments: arthritis, osteoporosis, diabetes—you name it, and Mama Kim had a medication for it. From 6:00 to 9:00 p.m., her phone would be busy, as she would call the various other women from her church group, and they would all discuss their ailments and medications for hours.

No, really. Hours upon hours. Every other word was "huh?" because they were all going deaf. Some of these women could not hear a .30-06 rifle shot if it was in their front yard at 3:00 a.m.

It was a predictable circle of women: Mary Frank, Florene, Reba, and Myrtice. Every night. I knew this because we all went to church together. Mama Kim sat in the same place every Sunday because there was a memorial plaque with Daddy Kim's name on her spot. Nobody sat there but her. The best thing about church with Mama Kim was the slices of bologna she had in her purse to give us when we got hungry.

One night, I was eating dinner at Neen's, and her police scanner made the telltale noise that Mama Kim was making a phone call. She had a cheap cordless phone, so any police scanner would pick up her calls. Usually, Neen would turn it off with a groan, because her scanner would be out of commission for the next two hours, drowned in a sea of Plavix, Advil, Bayer, insulin shots, and doctor visits.

Well, this particular night, Neen just kept eating, and the scanner stayed on. Mama Kim called Florene, and the conversation began normally. Medicine, pain story, doctor visit, pain story, who did not give when the offering plate came around, pain story. Then Florene interjected.

"Lucille, I got some bad news today."

"Oh Lord, what is it, Florene?"

After a forlorn sigh, Florene laid it out. "My niece has colon cancer. Yep. Starts chemo next week. Everybody is real tore up about it."

There was a long pause as Mama Kim processed this information.

"Florene, that is ridiculous. I ain't never heard of nobody getting colon cancer in their knees."

The best story about Mama Kim happened years before I was born, sometime in the late 1940s. My great-grandfather was working in the mill that day, and Mama Kim had the day off. She had just finished lunch at their house and was taking the table scraps outside, when a ghastly figure materialized on her screen door.

Sitting right in the middle of the door, in a menacing pose, was a praying mantis. "Devil horse" was what Mama Kim called them. She was very superstitious, and there was an old legend that if a devil horse spit in your eye, you would go blind. Mama Kim firmly believed this legend and was deathly afraid of devil horses—fainting, screaming, and sweating bullets as she ran through the house afraid.

She retreated back into her living room. With this devil horse laying claim to her front door, she could not leave the house. Who knew? Daddy Kim might come home, and it would spit in his eye! She could not call Daddy Kim, because he could not afford to take the time off. She called on a neighbor, Mr. Pickard. Luckily for Mama Kim, Mr. Pickard believed in the devil horse legend as well.

Bill drove the half mile to Mama Kim's driveway. He stopped in the road and slowly crept toward the house, so as not to startle the devil horse, because it could fly on you and spit in your eye. He crawled and hid behind a bush. He peered over the bush and saw the green spawn of Satan firmly entrenched on Mama Kim's door. Bill knelt back down, took a couple of deep breaths, and stood up to face the demon...with a 12-gauge shotgun. Bill walked within five feet of the door, took aim, and squeezed the trigger. The door and Mama Kim's front porch exploded in a hail of gunfire, and the devil horse disintegrated from the point-blank blast from the shotgun. Mama Kim came from her hiding place and surveyed the damage.

"Is it dead?!" Mama Kim asked.

Bill was happy to report that the devil horse was indeed dead and that her eyesight and the eyesight of the rest of Cassville was safe from this vermin forever. Daddy Kim came home five hours later to find his porch and front door completely destroyed. He ran into the house in a frenzy, thinking the worst.

The best compliment I ever heard bestowed on this wonderful woman was at her funeral. Mama Kim left us in 2000 at the ripe old age of eighty-eight. We were all sad to see her go, but when she looked up at us from her hospital bed and said "I cannot wait to see Dave again," we knew it was time.

Of the numerous people who came to pay their last respects, a local farmer approached me during the wake. It was the first time I had ever seen him when he wasn't covered in dirt. This was a guy who had a reputation around town, the kind of reputation that made people think twice about crossing him. He patted me on the back and looked at Mama Kim and said, "That's my old buddy right there. She was one of a kind, boy. You boys was lucky to have her, and I'm sure gonna miss her. I'll tell you one thing though. If she was a man, I would hate to meet him in a dark alley."

Nobody messed with Mama Kim.

CHAPTER 22

The End Game

OUR JOURNEY AT CASS GROCERY ended in August 2010. After years of standing behind the counter, my dad finally sold the place. While he was sad to see it go, fourteen-hour days and the constant stress of owning a business like that took its toll. It certainly was not all fun and games for him.

The last day was surreal. The guys on the benches were silent, as if someone close to them had passed away. Long-time customers shook their heads and hugged us, like we were moving to Thailand. Children inquired, "Are y'all leaving forever?" I walked the aisles that I walked so many years, memories rushing over me. How many times did I clean that shelf? I put up that display in 1994! My eyes became misty, and my throat was lumpier than grits in Ohio. Could it really be over?

Pumping my last gas, bagging my last gallon of milk, shutting the door to the walk-in cooler one last time, I could not help but smile. It was like graduation day, and I finally got my doctorate in humanity. The people I had come to know over the years would never truly leave me, as if they were classmates who I chose to keep in touch with after we turned our tassels.

The education that I received at Cass Grocery remains the most valuable to me, with all due respect to my teachers.

Seriously though, what could compare to this? Where else could you see these things? When I was in college, I talked to folks from all over the country on a daily basis. People from huge cities, suburbs, rural areas, foreign countries, and even Alabama. I never heard anyone tell me much that resembled Cassville or intrigued me as much as my own hometown.

The 30123 never ceases to amaze me.

Cassville itself has changed in recent years though. The population has grown with the influx of people running from the urban sprawl like the bubonic plague. There are a few subdivisions that would certainly be in the city limits if the town became incorporated. A few businesses have their eyes on property around there, looking to flatten the pine thickets and set up shop where I probably hunted squirrels at some point.

New faces pop up, often with a whimsical look that says "What is this place? How cute!" Voices lacking accent, colloquy, or influence. It makes me nauseous. I understand the attraction to the southern small-town, but these people cannot truly understand the sacred ground on which they stand. Their sweat did not fertilize the grass. Their lives are not engrained in the soil. Their voices do not echo off the walls of Cass Grocery.

Those voices that do echo, live on. The people who worked with me over the years have all become successful in their lives—raising families and making their way in this world. They went on to become engineers, linemen with the power company, teachers, coaches, and business owners themselves. Some served our country in the military. Many of our old customers still approach us about the good ol' days, letting us know about their lives and how much they miss seeing us.

There are times when I drive by the old place, and I can still see us out there. Sweeping up cigarette butts and watching the cars rust. Old men smoking and talking about the weather. Dad stocking shelves, Matt pumping kerosene with a smile on his face, and a younger version of myself carrying bags of potting soil to an awaiting tailgate. It was a simple way of life, and it was wonderful.

Dad went to work in education afterward, where he still remains today. He is no longer the boss, but he does not seem to care. I think he likes to walk out the door at 4:00 p.m. and not worry about ordering spark plugs in time or how many gallons of gasoline he pumped last week.

Mom still keeps us all in line and still knows everyone in the state of Georgia. When she goes to the grocery store, she is gone for hours because she talks to at least one person in every aisle. Her magnetic personality has never wavered.

Matt earned a bachelor's degree in finance from Ole Miss and works in sales. He is still a free spirit, but he has bills to pay like everyone else. That twinkle in his eye still exists, and I know the folks who live and work with him are enjoying every second.

We lost Neen in 2011. One day, she complained about feeling weak, and we all figured it was her sugar acting up. The weakness persisted, and a doctor visit revealed pancreatic cancer, a death sentence. It was ironic, because I remember her remarking how sad she was to see Patrick Swayze die so young from it only a few months prior.

"Such a talented, purty man," she'd lamented. Who knew she would face the same demon?

After a seven-month fight and several rounds of chemotherapy, Neen passed away. It really hurt to see her go, and I felt a darkness unlike ever before. A few days after her burial, I was doing yardwork at my house and feeling pretty sorry for myself. It was eerily quiet outside for a Saturday, I thought. Suddenly, I heard the telltale call of a dove from the roof of my house. I looked up and saw two of them sitting side by side, looking right at me.

I thought of Neen. How much she missed my grandfather all the years he was gone, and her love for all of us. Those doves seemed to be symbolizing her happiness to be reunited with him but letting me know she was not totally gone.

I didn't know if it was a sign from God or what, but I instantly felt peace.

Larry remained in our lives until he passed in 2014. I always made a point to stop by his house, just to get an update on how much he hated the Braves or random gossip about the trailer park. Larry would be propped up in his recliner, work boots on, chewing his Red Man. We still greeted each other with a bird finger, in accordance with our custom forged so many years ago. Despite his physical ailments, he cut his own grass and drove himself to the post office. He was as tough as they came.

His gruffness subsided as he aged. Larry loved us, and he expressed it during his last years. I sure miss him, and I know he is watching over us with Neen and everyone else who has gone "up yonder."

As for me, I am practicing law and carving my own niche in the universe. My days are filled with child support worksheets, probated wills, juvenile delinquents, and car wrecks now. I sit in courtrooms in my coat and tie, often wishing I was still changing oil and talking about the bass that Bill Dance caught in Nickajack Lake. My career is rewarding in its own right, but I do miss the interactions I had with customers at the store.

Laura, my wife, and I welcomed Elizabeth into our lives in 2015, and my daughter is blossoming each day. Life has been re-defined for us, and we love it. When she can understand and com-prehend life outside of bottles and diapers, I will teach Elizabeth about this place. She will know about Cassville and the people who I came to know as the best on earth. The mechanics, the farmers, the teachers, the characters, criminals, and loafers who called this place home.

Hell, I might even teach her how to git on it.